THE SOCIOLOGY
OF
LITERARY TASTE

THE SOCIOLOGY
OF
LITERARY TASTE

by
LEVIN L. SCHÜCKING

THE UNIVERSITY OF CHICAGO PRESS

The University of Chicago Press, Chicago 60637
Routledge & Kegan Paul Ltd., London, E.C.4
The General Publishing Company, Don Mills, Ont., Canada

Translated from the German *Die Soziologie der literarischen Geschmacks-Bildung* (first edition, Munich: Gebr. Paetel, 1923; second edition, Leipzig: B. G. Teubner, 1931; third edition, Bern: A. Francke AG Verlag, 1961)

First English translation, by E. W. Dickes from the second German edition, published 1944 in Great Britain by Routledge and Kegan Paul Ltd.

International Standard Book Number: 0-226-74100-1
Library of Congress Catalog Card Number: 66-12708

CONTENTS

Contents

PREFACE

THE basic idea underlying the present book is that the concordance of liking evoked by certain works of art, the concordance of liking which we call taste, is due to something other than a simple excellence inherent in the quality of the work itself; rather is it the product of a complex process in which a variety of forces—some ideological, some highly material—contend with one another and ultimately produce something that is itself far from immune to the actions of chance. The description in the present work of the processes in question is undeniably sketchy—a fact of which nobody is better aware than the author himself; for all that, however, there does seem to be room for such a work in so far as attempts to examine the subject of artistic preferences from such an angle are virtually non-existent. Actually—if we disregard a version dating back to 1923 which aroused little interest—this essay did not really appear in the bookshops till its publication by Teubner in 1931. It was ultimately destined to be translated into the following languages: Russian (Academia Publishing House, Moscow, 1928); Slovak (Trnava, 1943); English (London, 1944); and finally Spanish (Mexico–Buenos Aires, 1950).

After a generation it was the house of Francke in Bern that suggested it should be put before the reader, freed from certain markedly dated matter in what may be termed its illustrative material, and now the English version, for some time out of print, appears in a second edition.

Use has been made of the opportunity thus presented to

expand certain lines of thought and amplify certain illustrations already to be found in part in the author's essay entitled 'Fehlurteile' (Faulty Judgements) (*Essays*, Wiesbaden, 1948). It is hoped that certain points will thus be made to emerge more clearly and that the undiminished relevance of the work to the time in which we live will become even more apparent.

I

CONTEMPORARY TASTE
AND THE SPIRIT
OF THE AGE

The phenomenon of change in taste. Explanation from natural science in Brunetière.

THE history of literature, and particularly the history of art, has concerned itself hitherto almost exclusively with the work of art and the artist. The question of the development of artistic taste in the public, its 'how and 'why', has scarcely been touched upon. The result has been that certain developments in artistic life in recent decades have baffled the majority of observers. The nature of the change in taste that has made its appearance seems mysterious and fateful to many people, and to some a sign of a general collapse which they bring into the closest connexion with the submergence of their political or social ideals. But things are not so strange as they sometimes seem, provided that we view them in their true historic and sociological environment.

An attempt at the methodical explanation of the great upheavals in the life of literature was made by the famous French critic and historian of literature Ferdinand Brunetière. But his *Evolution des Genres dans l'Histoire de la Littérature* (1890) appeared at a time when the world was so thrilled by the achievements of the natural sciences that it was all too ready to see in the explanation which Darwin and his successors had found for the processes of nature the key also to the problems of intellectual life. Thus Brunetière saw a repetition of Darwin's Origin of Species in the development of the fine arts and of literature, with the rise from simple to complicated forms, the branching out into special generic forms, and the surprising progressions of youth, perfection, ripening, exhaustion, decay, and dissolution, as seen, for instance, in the history of the drama: he split up art into living genera, and imagined that he could apply to these in a large measure the Darwinian principles of selection.

In doing so he overlooked the fact that this was associating together things that in reality were not comparable and that had only apparent similarity with one another. On one side was life propagating itself independently through pro- creation or the sowing of seeds; on the other creation de- pendent on human thought. The life of art certainly has at times a measure of superficial similarity with the life of nature, in which the struggle for existence is the dominant principle; but it is not the genera, still less the individual works of art, that are at issue with each other—that can never be more than a simile—but the tendencies. Brunetière thinks that a particular genus, such as the drama, may at a particular time be without inner vitality and may therefore expire; but this, again, is pure mysticism. It is not the works of art or the forms that decide between themselves, but human beings. But in the life of human beings the change of forms plays an immense part, not only in relation to art but, as everyone knows, in relation to articles in daily use, to dress, and to a thousand other things of which it is impossible that all should be compared to the 'species' of living nature.

Apparent dominance of a contemporary taste
Thus it is difficult to consider art in entire isolation; yet it is here that, in many respects, this change is most striking. The conventional history of literature devotes remarkably little attention to the question why, to take a few examples at random, Schiller placed a man like Fielding among the

greatest classics; Byron's narrative verse, to-day no longer read, sold in thousands of copies on the day of publication; and a lock of Jean Paul's hair was regarded by thousands in Goethe's time as the most precious of relics. Those who do ask this question sometimes dispose of it too summarily, blaming the art of these persons, as rendered out of date by its primitive psychology or its lack of sincerity and depth of feeling or its facile garrulity. But if the readers of that period could be shown the art of our own, they would certainly not feel it to be an advance, such as they would be bound to recognise in the electric light as compared with the oil lamp or the railway train with the stage-coach. They might abandon the defence of the weak passages in the work of their contemporaries, but they would point to other passages that seemed to them of more value than all the art of the following period. In short, the difference that usually divides the older living generation from the younger in judgement of art would show itself here in a greatly accentuated form.

Even in regard to the so-called classics, complete agreement would be difficult to obtain. To begin with, it is an illusion that there can be any art that is more or less withdrawn from human differences. Our own feeling is that Shakespeare, for instance, was belittled for centuries. Similar cases in the fine arts are well known. The reader of Lord Chesterfield's letters to his son sees how a man who was the very embodiment of the *bon goût* of the eighteenth century has so radically different a judgement from ours, not only of literature but of the fine arts, that when his son asks him whether he should take the chance of buying a few Rembrandts cheap, he replies that the opportunity is not worth taking, since the artist in question painted nothing but caricatures.

Even where the artist's position is to all appearance un-challenged, even in the case, for instance, of Goethe, the keen observer may recognise a process similar to the phases of the moon, a continual waning and waxing of popularity. And it may be clearly seen that even where the enthusiasm is constant it is far from being felt for the same aspects of the same objects. The Elizabethans—that is to say, the public, not so much the *literati*—were certainly aware of Shakespeare's greatness, but it is clear that they praised in Shakespeare's art quite other things than we do. To take yet another example from the fine arts, anyone who reads the delighted descriptions which Bettina von Arnim gives in her efforts on behalf of the painter Blechen, who had just become so famous, will be astonished to see how little mention there is of the merits on which the critics of our own day base the outstanding rank of that painter.

All this points to one and the same phenomenon, that of the dominance of a particular taste at a particular time. This shows itself most plainly in the changing styles in the fine arts, and that is why in modern times, so strongly influenced by the fine arts, we have become accustomed to giving generalised descriptions to whole cultural periods. We talk nowadays of the period of the Renaissance—a phrase which to the generation that grew up so recently as in the 'sixties and 'seventies of the last century usually denoted a particular style of architecture. The idea of the Gothic Age is so largely disconnected now from the ogive that 'Gothic man' has become a favourite phrase of late among students of the philosophy of civilisation. And already the term 'era of expressionism' is coming into general use.

The connexion with the 'Spirit of the Age'
But how far is the artistic style of a period an intrinsic necessity? To no question has the reply become so much a matter of course as to this one. There was a time when every third paper one took up was informing its readers of the interconnexion existing in this respect. Art, one read, is the finest expression of contemporary feeling. Those who understand the language of form, especially in the fine arts, learn from it the most about the thought of the period. Man's attitude to things, his ethical valuations and his emotional preferences, are carried over into the direct expression in the arts of things perceived through the senses. Art is a sort of seismo-

graph that registers the slightest deviations from an existing intellectual point of rest. Such was the theory. It was held that in art, and above all in the fine arts, the Spirit of the Age gains embodiment and shape: a man of truly sensitive perception can deduce the whole intellectual life of a period from its art, as some nature-healers profess to read the whole state of the body in the eyes. How widely that view was held was shown by the report of one of the leading German newspapers on the Reichsgericht trials at Leipzig after the nationalist 'Kapp Putsch' in 1920. It said: 'Nothing more symbolical could have been found for the trial than the great hall in which the court sat. All that parvenu rubbish plastered over the walls—mendacious, inexpressibly affected, blind to the will to form that wells up unconsciously from the depth of the people! Anyone who looks at the state hall realises intuitively why the war and the collapse came, why there was a Kapp Putsch.'

Yet, tempting as it is to regard the art of a period in association with the other intellectual manifestations of the period, this is to take too simple a view of things. For there are many pretentious halls of state which in the author's view are no less 'rubbishy' than the one at Leipzig, in the capitals of European and American countries which had little part in the first war and no collapse, still less a Kapp Putsch. Such chiromantic art criticism as this need, of course, be no more than an exaggeration of a fundamentally correct idea. And does not the truth of the idea show itself in its pragmatic working-out? Goethe once said that that is truth which helps man forward. But what has helped forward our art, and especially our architecture and in architecture the building and internal arrangement of churches, so much as the establishment of the view that it is a sin against style to cling to rigid traditional forms? It is now felt, for example, that Gothic art was the expression of the life of the Gothic man, so that the art of to-day should not pride itself on building churches and altars in correct Gothic style, but must reflect the man of to-day in its language of form.

While, however, we owe new life in the most various fields to this idea, that does not place it above all critical examination. Particularly in the life of art, for reasons that can be understood, suppositions that were only partially correct have often led to the most wonderful results, as is evidenced, for instance, by the conception of the past in the history of the Renaissance or of the Romantic style, or in the history of literature by the forgeries of Ossian. Thus, if the style of art of a period is described without reservation as the embodiment of the 'Time Spirit' (Zeitgeist) or spirit of the age, it must be permissible to feel some doubt as to what exactly this spirit of the age is.

The Spirit of the Age and social groups

It is a striking fact that it is always so much easier to reduce the Time Spirit of past periods to a formula than to do so for a contemporary world. It is certain that the attempt involves a certain risk of question-begging. It is very easy to adduce as part of a demonstration the very thing that has to be proved. The spirit of the Gothic period, for instance, is first deduced from its art and then rediscovered in its art.

A follower of the philosophical outlook so highly developed in Germany would be sure to shout us down here, declaring that we have no problem here at all, that it is obvious that art corresponds to a particular *Weltanschauung* or general outlook, and that this *Weltanschauung* is what is meant by the spirit of the age. For such people art is primarily a bearer of ideas. 'The history of literature', says Hettner, for instance, 'is the history of ideas and of their scientific and artistic forms.' We may leave aside the question whether it is true that in the last resort all artistic forms presuppose ideas in Hettner's sense. But if the conception of philosophy is assumed to be substantially covered by Dilthey's tripartition, as a view of the world, a valuation of the world, and principles of action in life, the question arises at once: Which sociological group is meant? For any observer of the community as a whole quickly sees that in respect of view and

6

valuation of the world and principles of conduct the community varies very fundamentally within itself. To-day we no longer see things as simply as Herder, who conceived the spirit of the age as 'the principles and opinions of the most clear-sighted and most intelligent men'. The groups are too varied for their thinking to be brought so simply within a common formula. The most that can be done—if we disregard the regulation of such matters, if we disregard the 'socialist realism' enforced from above in Communist societies—is to distinguish groups.

To begin with, religious differences play a part in these groups. But apart from these, there are other groupings. The most outstanding are those produced by social differentiation. The varied social atmosphere results in varied social ideals. But which of these are the true expression of the time? Obviously, in talking of the spirit of the age, people have in view the more or less closely held common stock of ideas of a particular group which is regarded as the dominant formative group.

But even this conception is not wholly free from ambiguity. If what is meant is the class to whose will and resources advance in social life is due, this class is by no means always identical with the mainstays of art and science. Consider, for instance, the state of things in England at the outset of the eighteenth century, when the rise of the middle class was slowly taking place. The view and valuation of the world and the principles of conduct were entirely different at that time among the Puritan middle class and among the aristocracy. As a rule the social ideals of the two classes were sharply contrasted. But posterity held that in many respects, in regard, for instance, to marriage and family life, the ideals of the middle class were much the higher. In the course of time, these ideals gradually won through. Yet in this period science, and especially art, were mainly supported by the aristocracy. The leaders in science and art did not, indeed, spring from the aristocracy, but they found in it their main support and encouragement.

Or, consider the conditions in pre-Hitlerite Germany. Who then led? The workers could certainly make a strong claim to be at that time the formative class. For many progressive ideas, true cultural aims, some of them born among the bourgeoisie but more or less rejected by it, such as the whole complex of ideas of pacifism, or the rescue of the artisan from the domination of the machine, the working class was the true standard-bearer. In these fields it was 'in league with the future', as Ibsen said. But even its best friend would hesitate to maintain that, up to then at all events, it could be regarded as the dominant formative class. In view of the lack of interest among the great mass of manual workers in purely intellectual questions, which will only gradually disappear with the improvement in their economic situation, it can scarcely be claimed that advance in the fields of science and art, or in that of social life, is mainly dependent on the working class.

This makes one thing particularly clear: there is no such thing as a spirit of the age; there are only, so to speak, a series of Spirits of the Age. It will always be necessary to distinguish entirely different groups, with differing ideals of life and society. The question with which of these groups the dominant art of any period is most closely connected depends upon various circumstances, and only the dweller in a Cloud Cuckoo Land will make the answer to it dependent on purely ideal factors.

II

THE SOCIOLOGICAL MEDIUM
OF LITERATURE IN
THE PAST

VOSSLER, that witty historian of literature, says somewhere
in his book on Dante: 'Science and the fine arts may require
a rich economic soil. But imaginative writing is a flower that
flourishes merrily among rocks and ice, in frost and storms.
It is affected by the history of States and of wars only in so
far as they fill the imagination and appeal to the emotions of
peoples.' And Renan, in his book *L'Avenir de la science*, goes
even farther, or almost so, when he shows that the periods of
great political and social storms and upheavals are just those
that give life to great and fruitful new ideas. Among the
many examples he quotes in evidence of this, he points out
that it was actually in the time and partly under the yoke of
Napoleon that Germany passed through her classic period in
philosophy and art.

But the history of literature, regarded in its sociological
aspect, teaches us to view generalisations of this sort with a
certain mistrust. Let us confine ourselves in what follows to a
few fields of the immeasurable region open to us, to those
fields which have borne specially rich fruit, and let us see
whether they can serve as examples.

We quickly find that it is true that economically rich soil is
not in itself enough. Were it the one thing needed, there

would be periods during which the peasant would be bound to develop the finest art. The case is not so simple as that. Roses are not planted in cow-dung.

Is it to be inferred that creative literary activity is independent of material circumstances? Does it exist entirely apart from these? That might conceivably be asserted of certain popular forms, but certainly not of any great art or any art that bears an individual stamp. Just as in natural history the characteristics of fauna and flora can only be recognised in association with the peculiarities of the locality, so in the history of literature existence and colouring and individuality proceed largely from the sociological soil from which the literary creation springs. To keep to our picture drawn from organic nature, it may even be said that, for several centuries, imaginative writing was a sort of lovely plant parasite, growing on the main stems that overshadow state and economic life. In other words, the history of literature is in large part the history of the beneficence of individual princes and aristocrats.

The singer goes with the king, not because both live *auf der Menscheit Höh'n*—'on the peaks of humanity'—but because the king is the only person with the means to support the singer. But that means that the person supported is in receipt of support, and, consequently, must not forget his duty of gratitude. This had far-reaching consequences. The important part played by Gothic and Danish themes in heroic sagas—the enthusiasm shown for the old Danish kings in the Anglo-Saxon Beowulf—must surely be directly or indirectly related to the fact that in such places—in Denmark and in the Gothic castles that is to say—a very great deal had always been done for the epic bard. As against this the fact that hardly anything in the way of a truly genuine Anglo-Saxon saga has come down to us leads us necessarily to suppose that the little Anglo-Saxon courts of the Heptarchy and their predecessors were somewhat niggardly in their treatment of the court minstrel—the Scop. Where greater largesse prevails the singer makes it his task to glorify the deeds of the king and of his followers, among whom he must reckon himself. He sees himself as the mouthpiece of the court and like a modern poet laureate strikes his lyre on any festive occasion. If that is no longer the laureate's *forte*, it is at least incumbent upon him to make himself the prophet of the creed of the ruling powers; to be conservative and a man oozing loyalty.

In the Middle Ages much of the principal art kept entirely within the general outlook of the bread-giver. Consequently both the bright and the very dark sides of that outlook are plainly discernible. The world is seen through the spectacles of the feudal lord; there is no feeling for the little man and no respect for physical labour. The life of the poet in that age required no small measure of capacity for submissive acceptance of 'that state of life, unto which it shall please God to call' him, and while the moral backbone of the economically dependent seems to have been the product of a more recent development, it may be imagined that a defiant and independent mentality was not to be tempted into that specially precarious position. How bitterly did Walther von der Vogelweide suffer, by his own confession, from the fact that nature had not provided him with the good elbows needed for keeping abreast of competitors at the Thuringian court!

These difficulties might occasionally be lessened by the fact that the poet, living within the circle of interests of his princely patron, was naturally drawn into his way of thinking, and conversely that an understanding Maecenas permitted his protégé to go his own way in his art and took pleasure in playing the part of simple protector. But how often, nevertheless, must some difference of view between the two have poisoned the whole relation between them! Think of Petrarch, who yet, as the most celebrated poet of his day, enjoyed an entirely exceptional position. Into what difficult situations he was brought by the simple fact that the poet could not support himself by the sale of his works to the public! For twenty years he was supported by the Colonna family; then, when Rienzi achieved his dream of the revival of the Roman Republic, Petrarch carried on in his support a bitter polemic against the tyrants of Rome—those same Colonnas. Later he lived for a considerable time with the terrible Visconti family, at Milan.

Elsewhere, with the general understanding less, the conditions were still worse. Chaucer had his Visconti—the unscrupulous John of Gaunt. He ate the bread of a court at which French taste and the rather stale theories of love of past centuries were still accepted; and a good part of his literary activity ran on these lines. They still left room for the play of his sense of grace and elegance, his taste and wit and irony, but not for the real element in his popularity, his wonderful sense of the Thing as It Is, which made him at the end of his life the most vivid portrayer of the Middle Ages. But by then his relations with the court had probably grown far less intimate, and it may be that these descriptions in the *Canterbury Tales* were written for recital to an audience of burghers which tended at times to favour a markedly robust humour.

Such examples might be multiplied. In all of them the principle that he who pays the piper calls the tune meant that attention had to be paid to the likings of the patron.

This patronage loses little of its importance as determinant of aims through its incomplete exclusion of other possibilities. For the same reasons as in the Middle Ages it continues through the Renaissance period, though in rather different forms. The effort is made to strike the note regarded as ideal in the highest circles. Thanks to his social standing, the aristocratic employer is the aesthetic arbiter. It is a piece of good fortune to achieve entire agreement with him. 'What I have done,' writes Shakespeare in the dedication of his *Rape of Lucrece* to his patron the Earl of Southampton, 'is yours; what I have to do is yours.' This might be interpreted as polite phrasemaking, but that would be quite mistaken. We know how powerfully the aesthetic taste of a small aristocratic class was able at that time to impose itself in the field of true literature, in which the drama was not then fully counted.

Perhaps it would be scarcely possible to find a better example than this literature of Shakespeare's time of the extent to which the character of the work produced depends on the sociological soil on which it grows. The thing that strikes every reader to-day is the difference between the vivid Elizabethan drama—which in its best examples stands still as nobly as on its first day, speaking directly to us, and appearing imperishable through the vitality of its psychology and the verisimilitude of its representation of life—and the poetic literature, or the narrative literature, of the same period, which, in spite of the poetic talent it reveals, seems to us centuries older, because it lives in a world of ideas that no longer has anything in common with our own.

The main reason for this difference is that the determining sociological factors differ in the two cases. Pure literature was dominated at the time by the social group of the aristocracy. Anyone who wished to get his works printed did well to seek the patronage of a great lord; anyone who wished to secure any return from the printing secured it only in the form of the gracious presents made in return for enthusiastic and fulsome dedications.

Indeed, the poets of that epoch largely obtained their sustenance in their patrons' castles, where they then, at occasional meals, sat 'below the salt', that is to say among the servants; not exactly a place of honour.

The effect of these conditions on the character of art is manifest. In striving for the approval of the great lord, an approval which is made visible by his acceptance of the dedication, the writer is confined within the range of the lord's cultural ideals. The didactic tendency aimed at has only an aristocratic world in view. Thus Spenser, the greatest poet of that age, says of his greatest work, *The Faery Queen*, that its aim is 'to fashion a gentleman or noble person in virtuous and gentle discipline'. This, naturally, can be done only within forms that are in harmony with the other ideas of that group—a group that strives to distinguish itself from the common herd in language, style, clothing, bearing, and behaviour; a group, moreover, whose taste, in accordance with its whole training, seeks association with the antiquity of which the common people have no comprehension, strives after difficult and artificial forms, is esoteric, abominates realism, despises simplicity, and goes in search of humanism and culture.

Quite different is the position of the theatre in that period. The Elizabethan playwright is no longer dependent on the benevolence of a single patron. It is true that the various companies of actors describe themselves as in the service of great aristocrats, but this is no more than a formality rendered necessary by certain provisions of the law. It has also to be admitted that the plays of that period have in the main an aristocratic outlook, which shows itself especially in belittling the burghers. But this does not by any means imply that, like other literature, they are written to suit the aristocracy, any more than Hauptmann's *Weavers* was written for a public of Socialist workers, though the characters are revolutionary in spirit. In reality the influence of the sociological group plainly lay in this case in quite a different direction from that of the group that determined the taste in *belles lettres*.

It would, of course, be wrong to seek it at the other pole of social life, in the company of the noisy rowdies of whom we read so much in the descriptions of the Elizabethan stage: it certainly lay nearer an enlightened circle of jurists, physicians, and so on, from whose professions, as we know, came eager visitors to the theatre. But the thing that is certain is that the voice of a wide public played its part here.

This provided quite other possibilities. New fields lay open. An infinitely wider sphere of activity showed itself. Literature was written no longer with an eye to the approval of a particular aristocratic patron, who might easily demand, in consequence of his conservative outlook, that traditions should be respected; and the work of the artist was no longer directed by a small and exclusive social group, whose atmosphere was the breath of his life. The artist depended instead indirectly on the box-office receipts, and directly on the theatre managers who ordered plays from him.

But in the theatre the works that won applause were precisely those which through their closeness to life and their realistic psychology were bound to be foreign to the taste of the aristocratic world. Thus the shackles of tradition could here be struck off and a wealth of varied talents could find scope.

Much depended, however, on the composition of the public in this theatre and on the latitude the various groups allowed each other. In this respect the conditions in England, which had always been liberal, were clearly different, for instance, from those in France. No more telling example of this effect of the social outlook on the determination of taste could be found than Voltaire's attitude. An English critic had praised the natural expression in the line in *Hamlet*—

Not a mouse stirring.

'What?' replied Voltaire. 'A soldier may reply like that in the guard room, but not on the stage, before the highest persons in the nation, who express themselves in noble language, and before whom a similar language is required.' The nature of the classic style shows itself surprisingly clearly here as a product of court society.

In Shakespeare's time things were different in England in every respect. A particularly benevolent fate had already provided for Shakespeare by placing the actor's talent in his cradle. This enabled him to acquire a secure living at a theatre where a sort of socialisation brought such rewards to the principal members of the company that they were entirely independent of the favour of the aristocratic world. Not all men were so well off. The conception of intellectual property was only half formed at that time; the writer for the theatre received a good deal less than the actors. We may thus attribute to material considerations the fact that Shakespeare's most gifted forerunner, Thomas Kyd, the author of the most fascinating tragedy of the time, the *Spanish Tragedy*, on whose original *Hamlet* Shakespeare almost certainly based his play, abandoned the popular stage and went over to the aristocratic art. On the popular stage Kyd's real and exceptional talent had found scope in plays that exercised great influence on later literature. He had won the applause of the crowd by his extreme dramatic tension, by his essays in profound psychological motivation, and by a treatment in gloomy, mysterious colours.

But these are not the aims of the classic art that finds its supporters in moneyed and aristocratic and academic circles. Thomas Kyd went over to those circles, probably because the poor devil had suffered as was then usual—had been robbed of the material fruits of his work. He set himself to translate a tedious classicist tragedy by Garnier, a work possessing none of the merits just mentioned but in harmony with the cultured taste of his patrons. The case is no more remarkable than many others from that time to our own; purely material circumstances may determine which of two competing tendencies profits by the adhesion of a man of outstanding talent. The pursuit of bread leads the artist away from the course his talent indicates.

The influence on literature of the social power of the aristocratic group, restricted to some extent, for the reason here given, only in the theatre, continued plainly in English literature down to the eighteenth century. Only then did a real reading public develop on a wider scale. In place of the patron came the publisher. His first appearance amounted to a sort of intermediate stage, since the publisher depended on subscriptions, which for a good part of the eighteenth century were the main feature of the more important publishing ventures; the publisher thus depended on the personal relations between the author and individual patrons. Subscription issues have rightly been called a sort of collective patronage.

Among the first great publishers of the eighteenth century in England, men like Dodsley, the continued powerful influence of the aristocracy is still manifest: they were often advised by scholarly members of the aristocratic world. Only gradually, with the diminishing influence of the aristocracy in social and political life and the growing economic and social importance of the middle class, did another public grow up and conditions begin to resemble those of modern times. In this respect England, thanks to her political liberty, was well in advance of the Continent. In France, for instance, the new development proceeded a good deal more slowly, because the work of the publisher had inadequate legal protection, suffered from rigorous censorship, and was supported by an insufficiently wide public. Pirating was universal, and readers were few. Compared with the return obtained by writers of later times, the yield from the literary work of Rousseau, Diderot, or the Abbé Prévost, was miserable. The author of the *Nouvelle Héloïse* gained not much over £1,000 from the whole of his life's work, and the others were in straitened circumstances throughout their lives. So much the more essential was the continuance of the protection of a patron, with all that it involved.

In England the conditions were substantially better. With his own sharpened sense of economic necessities, Oliver Goldsmith (1730–1774) makes that plain. It is not difficult, he says, for a really efficient writer to become rich if he sets out to do so. He remarks at the same time on the great change that had contributed to liberate the writer from the oppressive and humiliating dependence on the 'great' and to win for him 'the dignity of independence'.

Thus, if we venture to seek a fundamental principle for all those centuries for the formation of taste as a sociological process, we might perhaps say that the sociological soil must not be lost to view. The soil does not, of course, create the art. The mud does not create the eel as Aristotle thought, but the generalisation no mud, no eel would be fairly near the truth. What happens in this intellectual field does not differ greatly from what happens in the realm of natural science: an endless variability of creation is influenced in definite directions by a certain selection. For this selection we find of importance in the past the circumstance that it proceeds from the literary interest of groups in possession of economic and social sources of power, on which the creative artists are dependent.

Where the sociological soil is destroyed or seriously injured by any external circumstances, this injury extends of necessity to the art that it supports. If in wars and other storms we find art continuing to develop unhindered, the reason can only be that in these cases the sociological soil is simply untouched. The tremendous storms, for instance, of the Napoleonic era left entirely untouched the worlds in which literature had its being. The battles of Jena and Auerstadt, for instance, made little change or reduction in the German reading public, and book prices did not rise sufficiently to make it impossible for the legendary schoolmaster-enthusiast surreptitiously to put his Jean Paul into Napoleon's coach as the emperor drove past.

At other times, however, wars have had quite other effects —when the actual soil of the literature of the time has been affected so that the material conditions for its existence or its creation began to fail. This is shown on countless pages of the history of literature.

III

SHIFTING OF THE SOCIOLOGICAL POSITION OF THE ARTIST

IF we now turn away from the conditions of past centuries and consider more recent times and particularly our own day, again looking for the determining factors, at first sight everything seems to be changed. In earlier times the sociological soil is mostly plain to see, the influence of particular people of social eminence is manifest, and there are only a few obvious centres from which the sustenance of the arts proceeds. To-day there are clearly many sources—numbers of theatres, publishing houses, associations, a public of varied tastes, and, in brief, theoretically a thousand opportunities. Social dependence has also clearly gone: remember, for instance, how lamentably Emperor William II failed in his attempt to introduce a taste into Germany from above, by means of a court art. This failure gave many people the pleasant feeling that social power can in our day no longer influence the course of true artistic taste. The only question is whether here, as in other fields, the effective influence has not shifted to another social force.

For this various circumstances are responsible. One of the principal of these is the change in the social standing of the artist. In past centuries the position of the artist in society was never particularly good. Those, of course, who had reached the peaks of Parnassus always found ready and honoured acceptance in the highest circles of society. Lord Chesterfield, who may be taken as an embodiment of the aristocratic culture of the eighteenth century in its highest manifestation, expressly states somewhere that he always felt it a distinction to be in the company of such men as Pope or Addison. It strikes us to-day, however, as odd when we hear that in 1723 a comedy of Steele's enjoyed great popularity because the author was reputed to have an income of a thousand a year. Clearly there was nothing much in being a mere artist.

For a long time the son of a 'good family' was considered in some way to have lost caste if he became a professional writer or painter, and still more if he became an actor. To live by the pen was not very respectable. When Congreve, who had become the most famous of English dramatists, crossed the Channel, Voltaire called to pay his respects to him, and mentioned that it was Congreve's fame as a writer that had inspired the visit. Congreve astonished Voltaire by replying that he was primarily not an author but a gentleman. Voltaire at once retorted that he would not have sought the acquaintance of Congreve the mere gentleman.

This social outlook changed only very gradually. It is significant that, for instance, Lady Bradshaigh, an aristocratic admirer of Samuel Richardson, was so afraid of what her Lancashire friends would say of her corresponding with 'an author' that she kept the correspondence a secret as long as she could. When he sent her his portrait she altered his signature to Dickenson, to prevent the acquaintance from coming to light. Thomas Gray left a small fortune in the possession of the publisher of his *Elegy Written in a Country Churchyard*, considering that it was beneath the dignity of a gentleman to take money from a publisher for his 'inventions'. He shared this inhibition—a most profitable one for his publisher—with Gellert in Leipzig. Walter Scott always preferred to be known as a landed gentleman rather than as an author. At the outset of his career Byron indulged in some magnanimous gestures to his publisher, though later these did not prevent him from extracting more money from the publisher for his works than any other poet of the nineteenth century.

In this respect the circumstances have probably never been the same all over Europe. This is, indeed, actually one of the criteria by which the national cultures may be distinguished. Thus, even in the twentieth century the social valuation of the artist has been rather different on the Continent, rather higher, than in the Anglo-Saxon countries. If, however, one has regard to the great phases of development, these differences appear as no more than nuances. In the matter of the social standing of the artist it is very significant, for example, that in Germany at the beginning of the nineteenth century, and for a long time after it, many aristocrats who engaged in literary work felt it necessary to assume middle-class pen-names—Anastasius Grün, for instance (Count von Auerspreg), and Nikolaus Lenau (Niembsch, Edler von Strehlenau: an 'Edler' corresponds roughly to a baronet), and Halm (Baron von Münch-Bellinghausen). How the family of Annette Droste looked askance at her literary activities! How reluctant the Kleist family was to talk about its son of genius! In his wonderful description of the 'thirties of the last century in *The New-comes*, Thackeray shows Lady Kew, genteel to the bone, rooted in the ideas of the eighteenth century, exclaiming with indignation at the news that a painter has asked for the hand of her grand-daughter:

'An artist propose for Ethel! One of her footmen might propose next, and she supposed Barnes would bring the message. "The father came and proposed for this young painter, and you didn't order him out of the room!" '

Gradually a complete change set in. It was the natural consequence of the changed outlook on life associated with the rise of the middle class. Here again the way was led by England, where the political revolutions of the seventeenth century had begun to make great changes in the relative power of the classes, which had remained unaltered through many centuries. Since the 'Glorious Revolution' of 1688 it had been necessary for the Government to reckon with the factor of public opinion. Consequently writers who could influence public opinion were taken very seriously by the leaders of the State. They were granted sinecures and flattered. Subsequently the writers suffered some change for the worse for a while, but during the eighteenth century the belief grew in the power of the printed word. In France, too, the prestige of literature grew steadily up to the end of the century.

Gradually, too, the ideal of personality changed. The ideal cavalier in the eighteenth century was the man of society with exquisite manners. The upper middle class brought art and science into the place of honour; it regarded the deepening of the intellectual life and the artistic elevation of spiritual life as important objects of existence. Art had played in the life of the aristocracy the part of a decorative element; in the life of the independent-minded middle class it had the more exalted task of serving as herald and prophet of the highest and the profoundest thought of mankind. Under these circumstances its representatives also were accorded a higher place than formerly.

Byron, who with his aristocratic origin and interests sympathised in many things with the past, himself records the change, with some surprise. He writes in his diary on 24 November 1813:

'I do think the preference of writers to agents—the mighty stir made about scribbling and scribes, by themselves and others—a sign of effeminacy, degeneracy, and weakness. Who would write, who had anything better to do? "Action—action—action,"—said Demosthenes: "Actions—actions," I say, and not writing—least of all, rhyme.'

In this there is a good deal of the earlier outlook. But now figures like Byron's, seen in the Bengal light of romance, served to give the poet a higher standing. The poetic activity of a man who moved among the highest peaks of society elevated, so to speak, the whole craft. Anyone who assumed Byron's air of world-weariness, and adopted his way of tying his cravat, gained, as he sought to gain, a portion of the interest and the admiration felt for the poet-lord.

Goethe's social position also exerted a powerful influence. In literature itself the signs of the changed social standing of the writer made their appearance. It is particularly instructive to see how late the artist is in appearing in literature as an attractive figure. The hero in the romances of earlier centuries is a knight, a prince, a cavalier, an officer; sometimes in the eighteenth century a clergyman. When, from 1709 on, Addison and Steele began publishing the so-called 'moral journals', the *Tatler* and the *Spectator*, which quickly found eager readers and imitators all over Europe, they represented themselves to the public as a sort of editorial committee, but in doing so they assumed the guise of a landed gentleman, a jurist, a great merchant, a half-pay officer, and an 'elegant' from the world of gallantry. A writer or an artist would not yet have been considered dignified enough.

A hundred years later all this was changed. Interest centred, for the first time, in the artist. In Goethe's *Wilhelm Meister* the hero, characteristically, is something of an artist, and the greatest English novelist of the nineteenth century, Thackeray, in *The Newcomes* (1853), in many respects of all the novels the best documents of the 'thirties, also makes his hero an artist. The two novels had many successors, in which the newly revealed predilection of the dominant class is reflected. For this middle class, though originally it established its dominance on the ideas of common sense and naturalness, had fallen victim to all sorts of affectation, had become aristocratised and narrowed by a thousand conventions. Half conscious of this inner discordance, it nurtured a secret affection for the untrammelled existence, as it saw it, of the artist. He was the embodiment of the human freedom for which it longed but which it scarcely dared to approve openly, still less to practise. He was almost a higher type of human being.

Shifting of the Sociological Position of the Artist

In the second half of the nineteenth century the artist is gradually accorded a position of which no earlier century would have dreamed. Age-old aristocratic prejudices fail to withstand this development. Pen-names are thrown aside and the aristocracy now devotes itself openly to art, rejoicing if it is mentioned in connexion with artistic achievements. Börries von Münchhausen the composer of ballads lived in princely palaces and took a valet with him on his travels; from the end of the century he appeared in Germany and gave public recitals of his works, charging for admission—happy to be able to describe himself as an artist.

Naturally this process was accompanied by a great increase in the artist's self-confidence. It is not difficult to produce instances from earlier times in which witness is borne to artists' pride. For even antiquity was acquainted with the idea that the poet was a prophet, a seer, a vessel of divine inspiration, an idea that is closely associated with the elevation of poetry above science, which is allegedly only the child of poetry. The Renaissance had given new life to this notion and had ascribed to poetry the function of expounding the divine law. But here too—as was the case in the outlook of the neo-classicism that was to follow afterwards—the basic assumption was that poetry deepened knowledge and provided moral leadership. But when the intellectual and moralising element receded into the background during the romantic movement this finally marked the beginning of the artists' own self-ennoblement. The most daring expression of this last is to be found in the words of F. W. Schlegel: 'What man is among other creatures on the earth the artist is among men. He is the Brahmin of a separate caste. Yet it is not his birth that ennobles him but the free impact of his personality (*frei Selbsteinwirkung*).' It would be easy to compile a great garland of such statements from the time of the romanticists onward. 'The man who stands above all others, the poet,' declared the young Levin Schücking in an essay, as though it were a self-evident truth, and his friend Freiligrath claimed for the poet that he 'goes about the world in solitude with flaming brow'. Very similar views were heard at the same time in the rest of Europe. Tennyson, for instance, whose lyric diamonds were extracted from no great depth below the surface, advised the common man with priestly solemnity to give up the attempt to probe the poet's unfathomable mind with his 'shallow wit'. This attitude visibly gathered strength as the century proceeded. It was plainly visible at its extremest in France, very noticeable in England, faintest at first in Germany. In an age that levelled all external differences, the poet marked himself off from the common man even in his clothes. Velvet coat, a flowing mane, and if possible special headgear, served to set apart many of these elect, especially the artists. Even in England, so exceptionally correct in externals, traces of this habit were to be found, though they did not succeed in effectively establishing themselves in face of convention.[1]

Thus the picture slowly changed. In the eighteenth century the wise Shaftesbury had expected almost a new flowering of literature from an increased 'personal dignity' in the status of the poet. His phrase proved prophetic. The sense of bearing 'the dignity of humanity', as Schiller said, in his hands made the artist capable of the greatest achievements. But gradually the artist's position shifted. He began to be enthroned above men, as the priest is enthroned above the faithful in church, and already intelligent people began to ask themselves, as happened as early as 1872 in a very acute article in the *Quarterly Review*, what effect this exaggerated artists' assessment of their function, this separation of their intellectual sphere from that of the ordinary man, would be bound to have in the end on art itself, how it would ultimately lead of necessity to a false relation between human and artistic values in the life of art, and in a different form would needs result in producing the artificiality and the estrangement from the natural and the popular which, it was

[1] It is significant that on the morning of the day on which Tennyson was to make his first entry into the House of Lords after the peerage granted to him as Poet Laureate, a friend called on him to urge him on this occasion at least to discard his customary poet's sombrero for the only correct wear, a top hat.

supposed, had been happily overcome in the romantic movement.

At first, it is true, there was not much sign of this in the ruling art. Tennyson set his hat but not his head against popular opinion. As his biographers almost unanimously relate, he always adjusted his own inner development—often almost by force—to the conception of what should be the nature of a poet who wants to give his people the bread of life in his art. Things were similar in France, where Victor Hugo altered the ending of his tragedy *Marion de Lorme* at the desire of the public and under the influence of Prosper Mérimée and Dumas.

How far from sovereign was the artist originally in Germany may be seen from many examples. How patiently in the literary society of the Tunnel the criticism of dilettantes was endured! The educated public had here immense power in its hands, and it would certainly be wrong to say that it always made wise use of it. This applies especially to its resistance to the entry of new ideas in the sphere of the drama. It seems to us to-day almost incredible that at the first production in Berlin of Ibsen's *Doll's House* the concession was made to the public of bringing Nora back into the doll's house at the end. It is difficult to say what is the more astonishing in this incident, the public aversion from new ideas or the deference to it of so furious a defender of all individual rights as Ibsen, who in permitting the change allowed the point of his problem play to be blunted.

The new conception of art that came with the fall of the aristocratic world radically changed the attitude of the artist to his times. It has at all times been natural to the artistic temperament to get rid of the uncomfortable sense of failure by simply throwing the blame on others, charging them with bad taste. In taking comfort from the thought that the work was too good, that, in Shakespeare's phrase, it was 'caviare to the general', the self-confidence so essential to creative work was maintained, and the author was preserved from torturing, galling, incapacitating doubts.

Thus it would be easy to collect instances from the sixteenth century onwards, and perhaps even from earlier times, of expressions of dissatisfaction from artists in which the public and the critics are charged with lack of understanding. Especially they are set down as uneducated. But what now came was something different, a conception of artistic creative work in which no regard was paid to the existing public and the writer had in view only the ideal reader. He was guided now only by his own taste and conviction.

It is not always realised that past centuries did not hold such rigorous opinions on the subject. Alexander Pope, for instance, was regarded in England almost throughout the eighteenth century as a poet of the very first rank. Yet when he had completed his chief work, the translation of Homer, a real marvel in the opinion of his contemporaries, he read it to his patron, Lord Halifax, in the presence of a large assembly; and, says Samuel Johnson, the noble lord interrupted him now and then to propose improvements. Such proceedings had been allowed for centuries without protest by the artists. Chaucer's famous disciple Lydgate evidently regarded it as entirely natural when his patron Duke Humphrey of Gloucester, brother of Henry V (1413–22), 'corrected' his manuscript; and we know of exact parallels to this in the life of Spenser, who was contemporary with Shakespeare. Shakespeare himself in sonnet 78 declares that his Maecenas 'mends the style' of others and in his *Hamlet* shows us a prince who instructs actors like an experienced director.

In France the conditions were similar to this even in the eighteenth century. Voltaire himself was essentially a writer for society, producing his works for a particular environment and accepting directives from it. He read his *Oedipus* at Sceaux in the entourage of the Duchess of Maine, and had no hesitation in paying a good deal of attention to the criticism and advice tendered to him in that circle.

This social pressure was not yet challenged, but it is easy

to understand what a burden it must have been for the artist. Voltaire learned from Pope, who in material respects was fairly independent, of the more tolerable character, at all events, of the similar slavery to taste in England; and he inferred very logically that the principal thing was to get together some capital. We know how he accordingly entered into financial speculations, not all of a very admirable character. But we see also that Voltaire was only able to give play to his real nature and talents when he had established himself on his own estate near Geneva.

At this time conditions were changing, through the development of publishing, and a few generations later there were no more naïve attempts by aristocrats to improve the work of the foremost writers of their time. The artist emancipated himself more and more effectively from his environment.

With surprising speed the artist now proceeded towards the goal of entire autonomy, no longer paying any attention to his public. Shelley declared at the beginning of the nineteenth century as an obvious principle and nothing new:

> Write nothing but what your conviction of its truth inspires you to write; you should give counsel to the wise, and not take it from the foolish. Time will reverse the judgement of the vulgar. Contemporary criticism only represents the amount of ignorance genius has to contend with.[1]

The measure of hostility to the great public that may be detected in this statement from a passionate political democrat could be paralleled by earlier examples; it now became the accepted belief of an important literary movement, which later spread throughout Europe, the 'aesthetic movement'. The springing up of this movement all over Europe was a natural result of a certain specialisation in every field and of the increased respect for art in certain groups. Their interest in art led them to occupy themselves with the elements of art on which its appeal depends. Its effect, they considered, on an educated taste cannot lie in things outside art, such as a

[1] E. J. Trelawny, *Records of Shelley* etc., 1878, Vol. I, p. 30.

morally uplifting or a stimulating subject. From this view came the cult of things that in the view of earlier generations were only the media of art—form, rhythm, tone, allusion, and so on. In earlier times these things had not been ignored, for poetry was not invented in the nineteenth century, but however highly they had been appreciated they had been considered only in conjunction with other factors that had been valued more highly. But for this new group, concerned only with cultured appreciation, there were no higher elements than these.

One of the first men in Europe to spread this view with any great success was Leigh Hunt. In the early part of the nineteenth century he continually expounded to his fellow-countrymen in learned periodicals the elements of the poetic achievement of such men as Marlowe, Spenser, or Milton. He had beyond question a keen eye for poetic beauties, but the things to which he pointed were largely elements of their art which Marlowe and Spenser and Milton would not themselves have regarded as the essence of their achievement.

In France this cult of the media of art was called *l'art pour l'art*—art for art's sake. It divorced art from all influence over life except the purely aesthetic, and so confined it within a sacred grove whose priests were the artists. Artist-priests performed their offices, often, like Gautier and later his emulator Oscar Wilde, entirely removed from the common herd by the extravagances in which they at times indulged. The ordinary man could not follow them, could not conceive why any sensible man should spend a whole day in the pursuit of the only right adjective or in the attuning of a couple of vowels.

The issue between these groups and the public was not hushed up but proclaimed. Another group, with Rossetti enthroned at its centre, came into existence in England with the aim of protecting the arcana of its art from the profane. Rossetti himself once drew a clear distinction between himself and Tennyson, who, he said, was always endeavouring to keep within 'the realm of the public'. All connexion with the public, it was assumed, weakens the priest for his service to beauty. The story is familiar of the opposition to the prevalent opinion into which the further development of this point of view drove Oscar Wilde, in whom, as Friedrich Brie wrote in his *Aesthetische Weltanschauung* (1921), 'the idea that the beautiful contains a higher morality in itself became the idea that beauty and art sanctify whatever is done in their name, so that the artist can do no wrong.'

The similar German movement, which came late on the scene, shows the same divorce on principle from the '*Bildungspöbel*' ('cultural mob'). The French talked of 'the five of us', to mark the narrow circle of the truly cultured; Rossetti shut himself off even as a painter by refraining absolutely, on principle, from holding an exhibition, and wove about his whole existence a veil that to his contemporaries seemed mysterious and romantic; and similarly the group around Stefan George long seemed to the curious to be wreathed in a cloud—a more or less merciful one, perhaps.

This segregation from the public did not in all these cases mean a cessation of dependence on the public. Even the priest, high as he stands above the crowd, needs the crowd if only as the *misera plebs contribuens*. Not only that; recognition and admiration give wings to the artistic imagination, and so it may not seldom be observed how, from the most intimate of needs, the public so proudly driven from the front door by Their Magnificences was cordially admitted by the back door.

Contact with the public was maintained through the critic. But the only recognised critics were those who had the entry to the arcana and had been initiated—persons, that is to say, who had been more or less won over to the group's aesthetic outlook. Such critics proceeded from the circles of the aesthetes with the same inevitability as from any other logically developed system. It follows also that each of these esoteric groups grew into a sort of mutual admiration society. The contemporary world wondered why the critics, who had usually represented a conservative taste, suddenly threw themselves into the arms of the practitioners of a new art. But it failed to take account of sociological processes.

IV

LITERATURE AND PUBLIC

The deepening of the cleavage between public and art through Naturalism

THE aesthetic movement in Germany was of no great importance. Of more note was the German movement of Naturalism. In Germany Naturalism (or realism) came remarkably late. In France its most eminent representative, Emile Zola, had written his most famous novels in the 'seventies; he sought admittance to the Academy in 1888. About the same time (1886) Tennyson, then an old man, indignantly hurled his lame imprecation (now of great historic interest) in *Locksley Hall sixty years after* against the new movement, which had already had in the 'seventies a potential leader in Henry James, who was related to it in many aspects of his character. Tolstoy's *Anna Karenina* was begun in 1874; Ibsen's *League of Youth* dates from 1869.

In Germany at that time the main buttress of art was a cultured middle class, largely made up of higher officials, which, mainly in consequence of the political stagnation that followed the victorious wars, restricted itself in every field to the careful guarding of traditions. The cultural leadership lay in the hands of this class, and it was able to point to fine work from Heyse, Storm, Baroness von Ebner-Eschenbach, and others, authors who in their origin and outlook were closely united to it; but it had little to offer in art to the universally increasing body of those who had been brought by the conditions of the period into a certain opposition to the past development.

The sense of the hollowness of the religious conceptions that continued to dominate the school and the life of the State; the struggle against the so-called points of honour of privileged classes; the increasing hardness of the conditions of existence, due to the growth of competition, as reflected in the growing importance of the women's question; the increase in the elements of conflict in social and political life, the acceptance of scientific methods in every sphere, the trivialising influence of the great cities—all these things combined to lead certain social groups into a passionate struggle in various fields of everyday life against what they felt to be empty phrases. Naturalism is the striving after truth at any price, even, if it must be, at the price of disgust. 'The veil of fiction' is torn 'from the hand of truth', in the determination to look life in the face and see things as they are, everywhere, and therefore in art as elsewhere. The path of art is no Sunday stroll through pretty country with a young flock, but an everyday pilgrimage that does not shirk the investigation of any site.

It was difficult for such a view to win through anywhere, and it was nowhere more difficult than in the Germany of that time. For the cultured elements of the country were largely rooted in socially and politically reactionary conceptions. Their artistic needs were still confined to the family circle; their ideas of decency and respectability corresponded to an economic order that was in process of dissolution, making it for them a moral duty simply to close their eyes to a large part of life. Thus it was only small groups of journalists in the great cities that took up the cudgels for the new trend in art. Many of these held extremely advanced political views and unconventional ideas in regard to religion, the family, and society, and not a few were personally at feud with the social classes that set the tone.

This happened about the end of the 'eighties. Here we have to do with the greatest wholesale change of taste for centuries, and in some respects of many centuries; here we have the root of all later developments. It would be very useful, therefore, to give a full account of these processes, revealing this movement not always merely in its works and in particulars of individual lives, but as a sociological current in taste. It would be useful to know which newspapers and periodicals went over to the new tendency, whether their political and denominational attitude played a part in this, how the capital and the smaller cities differed, and the east and the west, the south and the north, and what the satirical journals said. We need an inquiry into the views of particular social groups and professions, and especially of those persons, such as teachers or ministers of religion, who had in the course of their ordinary duties to take up a definite position in regard to cultural questions. We need an examination of the sales of books and the number of editions, both for the old and for the new advancing literature. We should sift the propaganda matter. We should further ascertain the attitude that the lending libraries took up, and the extent to which book clubs among the educated classes were influenced, what new circles were won over by the new literature and what old ones repelled by it. Information should finally be collected concerning the corresponding influence exerted upon reading groups and upon social activities connected with literature.

Such an investigation would yield very instructive results. It would show at the outset what extraordinarily violent opposition was offered to the penetration of the new ideas, the representatives of which were almost held up to personal odium. (Gottfried Keller, for instance, denounced Emile Zola as 'a quite common fellow'. He was obviously moved to do this because Germany did not yet enjoy the freedom in the representation of erotic subjects which was permitted to France. That freedom was only granted after Gustav Frenssen opened the way to it in his widely read novel *Jörn Uhl*, published in 1901. One might add that Henry James also spoke of Emile Zola as a 'common fellow' and described his *Nana* as 'unutterably filthy'—*Times Literary Supplement*, 16 Nov. 1962, p. 867.) It would show how at the beginning of the 'nineties there was a period during which every society, every club, every family resounded with passionate declarations by the representatives of the old ideas, to the effect that for thousands of years the artist had set out to represent not the true but the lovely and noble. Had not the very language been affected by this, since it spoke of 'heroes' of a story or a drama? Had not artists, for as long as men had given expression to thought, represented the dreams of humanity? Had not children been named after heroes and heroines of poesy—children whom their tender parents would fain have seen grow up into similarly radiant figures? And now was art to be invaded by inexorably accurate observation in place of loving enlightenment? Had not art in all ages implied selection? Had not fantasy been its highest achievement? And now was a 'cross-section of reality' to suffice? But all observations of this sort, which in conversation almost always took the form of 'but art ought . . .', 'but art must . . .', were demolished by the triumphant declaration of the new order that 'art has no "ought" or "must" but only a "will" '. That showed how much the new trend was indebted to the 'art for art's sake' movement.

The most compelling arguments in questions of art are the works of art themselves. But at first there were no great works of art in the new style in Germany. For a long time the admired masters were foreigners, particularly Ibsen, Zola, and Tolstoy. In place of German works in the new style there came a criticism of the old style, a criticism from which it was by no means easy for the public to judge of the valuable elements in the new art. Much of the German love of the doctrinaire was brought at first to the criticism of all that seemed contrary to the new programme in art. Many forms that were revived after a few decades, the historical novel, the ballad, all art that betrayed a tendency, fell victim to the naturalist St. Bartholomew's Night. Heyse was slaughtered, Schiller fulminated against. On the other hand

Hebbel and Kleist were honoured (in past generations they had achieved no more than a *succès d'estime*), and while Geibel, earlier a famous lyricist, was hurled from the throne with a great clatter, Annette von Droste was discovered in the obscurity of her rural retreat, and Mörike was raised up in triumph.

The revolution in taste extended to the satirical journals. In place of the polite stereotyped exaggerations that had been regarded as comic in the past, there now came 'true stories', mainly in the form of letters addressed to the periodicals (*Jugend, Simplicissimus*). It was possible to object that a story is no more comic for being true, but with the reader's increased sense for the real this condition did at least add to the attraction of the story.

Beginnings of the predominance of the fine arts

The programme that envisaged the mission of art as the representation of a coherent piece of reality was bound to meet with stronger opposition in literature than in the fine arts. Here it quickly achieved the most brilliant victories in Impressionism. Its pioneers threw bridges for thousands into a world until then unknown. It was seen that traditional ideals of beauty had obstructed the outlook rather than not. Discoveries like that of the heath by the Worpsweder School represented a landmark on the path of development for masses of people. The impediments that stood in the way of the enjoyment of the new art in literature fell away sooner in the fine arts because there no ethical considerations came into play. 'Witness to the nature of man', as the Danish critic of literature Georg Brandès described Zola's art, might seem insufficient or open to objection to many who expected from art the treatment of the valuable and unusual, but witness to the nature of Nature was welcomed with gratitude and unreservedly accepted as an enrichment of the world of the senses. The new principle, proclaimed by Flaubert, that the matter is unimportant, the treatment all-important, was most easily intelligible in this field. The impetus given to fine art in this way was, in point of fact, particularly striking, and the leadership it thus gained among the arts was unmistakable. For a long time past it had been dominated by literary ideas; now the situation was reversed.

Even men's language gave an impression of the much greater importance gradually acquired by the fine arts. In the first half of the century, when the talk was of art in general, it frequently referred to the poet. 'The man who stands highest, the poet,' said Levin Schücking. In exactly the same way Shelley spoke of the 'poet' in statements of principle, where at the end of the century the talk was of the 'artist' (most dictionaries still reveal nothing of the change) —a word that in the current language of earlier generations had been confined to those who practised the fine arts.

Cleavage in the public and set-back for the literary element in social life
Such partial successes strengthened the new movement as a whole, but the great educated public remained dubious and unsympathetic to naturalism as a literary innovation. Now, however, there came in Germany a change not before seen on such a scale, though it had had its forerunners in the aesthetic movement: the gulf between public and artist steadily grew. The reputation of a poet or author in periodicals and newspapers was often out of all proportion to his popularity among the public, because there was too great a divergence in ideals of art. What, for instance, was the size of the editions of Johannes Schlaf or of Arno Holz in this period? The critics were unanimous in acclaiming Detlev von Liliencron as the great new poet, but the public followed them only hesitantly and by ones and twos. It is significant that the relatively poor Germany of 1867 subscribed a sum of 180,000 marks to enable Ferdinand Freiligrath, the spokesman of the passionate political dreams of its youth, to return home from England, while a collection made just a generation later in 1897, for Detlev von Liliencron, yielded barely 1,000 marks. So greatly had the former appealed to the hearts of the cultured, so little the latter. It really seemed

as if a programme of art that was based on a deep ethical aspiration was able to hold human feelings in firmer bondage than that of naturalism at first succeeded in doing.

The gulf between public and critics that thus opened had the less prospect of being closed again by natural means, the more the sociological divisions in society grew. This 'society' in the narrower sense, that is to say the grouping formed by members of the upper class, in which the tone was set by the higher official with university training, was a conception incredibly seriously adhered to up to and beyond the end of the nineteenth century. To be able to move in that circle was almost everything, to be excluded from it almost annihilation. Much of its ceremonial was almost sacramental. Mere vestiges of it now remain. The last bond that held it together, that of the officers in the reserve, was severed by the Treaty of Versailles (1919). The idea of 'Gesellschaftsfähigkeit' or 'Social acceptability' in the old sense of that term can no longer be sustained; it has been equally impossible for the class with university education to maintain its privileged position at a time when the excellent first president of the German Republic, Friedrich Ebert, came from the saddler's trade and the highest posts in the State were filled by men who had not been to a university.

But the loosening of the old social bonds had been in progress long before this democratisation began. The shrinkage in the consumption of alcohol largely reversed the stimulus to sociability produced by the introduction of coffee into Europe at the end of the seventeenth century. Men's societies and unions died out, 'Stammtische' or café groups dwindled, the conception of 'social obligations', which had played so great a part among the ruling higher officials, shrank steadily, and everyone began to claim more freedom of choice in social life. On the other hand the purely professional associations and representative bodies grew in number and in the claims they made on the individual's time.

Among the changes that took place at the same time as this and in connexion with it was a complete change in the importance of the literary element in social life. The upper middle class especially had been closely associated with literature. The broadening and deepening of the influence of literary education had been the distinctive sociological mark of the period of the 'Aufklärung' ('Enlightenment'). It continued among the middle class in the nineteenth century, making further advance with the great achievements in literature. This process was not confined to Germany. Thackeray, in his description of the 'thirties, makes fun of the way in which the literature of that period could even invade the place due to politics. He gives a witty description of the way the Member for Newcome, the banker Sir Barnes Newcome, a shrewd, sober, heartless business man, with not the slightest feeling for literature, feels bound to angle for popularity by giving lectures on the *Poesy of Childhood* and the like.

Things were much the same in Germany. At that time there existed, not only in the capitals but in the provincial cities, numbers of big and little literary *salons* and societies, dating back in certain forms to the second half of the eighteenth century at the earliest, for the discussion of literary questions and new literary works over tea and cakes. Their members were not mainly young girls but very serious people, married women, government officials, judges, officers. For these literary associations were one of the main forms of social gathering, and literature provided the means of 'setting out the dominoes' for conversation. It also laid the foundation of the bridge that spanned the gulf separating the nobility from the higher bourgeoisie. The two classes now began to find common ground in shared intellectual interests.

Needless to say, young unmarried persons were also to be found here. For them literature has, naturally, always had a special significance since the time of the very first great prose story of European fame, the story of Lancelot of the Lake, over which, as Dante relates, Paolo and Francesca came so close together in spirit that 'that evening they read no more'. But in this later literary age it frequently occurred that a book provided the first incentive or gave material assistance in the formation of a lifelong union. The new literary work provided the neutral soil on which acquaintance was formed; here the opportunity was gained of securing from the other's judgement of men and things an insight into his thoughts and feelings, an insight likely to become the first bond between kindred souls.

To-day this path appears almost in a romantic light, now that young people no longer form a rose-coloured view of each other from surreptitious and often misleading glimpses of the partner's imagined mentality, gained in the course of a formal party or a reading with distributed parts, but secure a thorough acquaintance with each other in sport or in working together. In other words, literature has long ceased to be the main subject of conversation, still less the common ground of social life.

This is not the place for a consideration of the course of this development from the 'Biedermeyer' period to its end. It is sufficient to realise how plainly visible the change is. If about the end of the century a newspaper produced a supplement for the entertainment of its readers it was devoted as a matter of course to *belles lettres*. Its contents were literary, historical, artistic. This is no longer the case, and the reason is not at all the one sometimes given, that literary interests are looked after in special periodicals; the reason is that where in the past literary and historical interest was dominant, to-day in Germany its place has been taken by natural science, politics, social reform, and sport. It is just in the politically progressive newspapers that the purely literary element is noticeably neglected; the politically conservative newspapers pay much more attention to it. Fundamentally the school has passed through the same development. The education given by the old school, the humanist 'Gymnasium' or 'public school', was mainly historical and literary. To-day a number of new types of school devote themselves to other interests.

The splitting up of the public produced by all these things

is bound to show itself in its relation to art. To make the great change clear from a striking example, let us recall the composition, say, of the first-night audiences in Berlin even before the war of 1914–18. A well-known Berlin dramatic critic once gave a very subtle analysis of this audience—not, unfortunately, for the premières but for an ordinary performance. He brought to light various significant things—first, that the audience was the strangest mixture of thoroughly heterogeneous elements—local people who had a liking for this particular theatre, people who could get there easily by tram, visitors to Berlin who had seen the announcement of the play on the pillar-hoardings, and so on. The same was true, *mutatis mutandis*, of the whole of the German art public: it had not a trace of homogeneity. This did exist at a time when the uniformity of the course of education, of interests, and of conditions of life in the ruling class, and the possibilities of personal intercourse that existed before the growth of the great cities, of necessity produced a greater uniformity in taste. But the times when the 'educated person' was a type determined by only a few elements are over. A completely changed sociological structure has come into existence, with much the same relation to the old conditions as to present conditions in a small town with no industries, where the general tempo of existence is much more leisurely, the influence of the layman on art is still taken for granted, the level of education of the social leaders is still fairly uniform, their experiences are broadly the same, their conditions of existence and their economic situation similar, their political ideas not radically divergent, their other ideals not entirely opposed, and thus their demands on art not worlds asunder.

What is the result of this social splitting up on the life of art, and especially on the formation of taste? The result has of necessity been, in art as in other fields of human life, the leadership of those who feel themselves to be experts. But elements of another character also try to gain the ear of the public.

V

THE START OF NEW
TRENDS OF TASTE

The formation of aesthetic cliques

IN the layman's view the sociological process of the formation of taste is a sort of formation of aesthetic cliques. Somewhere, at some time, an artist follows the divine summons sent to him and, true to an inner urge, responsible only to himself and answering no call from the outer world, creates the work of art that is dictated by the ideal that floats before him. The work is brought into the light of day, it shows divergences from existing art, and accordingly it does not fit into the contemporary scheme of taste. But by virtue of its intrinsic propaganda power it gains friends, gains recognition, and thereafter affects the general artistic taste. So it seems to the laymen.

This conception is, of course, largely right. We all know of such cases, and it is especially easy to see how the enthusiasm for a new work of art, often accompanied and reinforced by a certain pride of discovery, gives wings to the propaganda from person to person which first paves the way for a change in taste. Once the German publishing firm of Diederichs enclosed a slip in every copy of one of its books, asking the reader to inform the firm what led him to acquire the book (a measure, incidentally, of which the book trade was subsequently to make extensive use), and it proved that an astonishingly large percentage had bought it on the strength of the personal recommendation of friends. Later, in 1926, the Leipziger Buchhändler-Börsenverein organised an extensive statistical inquiry on the same lines, with much the same result. Against 195 cases in which a particular book had been bought on the strength of a review, no fewer than 391 purchases were due to a friend's praise of the book. Since then much admirably exact research has been undertaken in this field. Admittedly this tends to show that most people who purchase books cannot be brought within any such simple category as the organisers of the first questionnaires so unhesitatingly assumed.[1] Even so their findings do not nullify the impression that the personal factor is extremely important in the formation of taste.

In the case of a contemporary innovation that is certainly so even more than in other cases; in this case the threads may be followed to the immediate circle of the artist's personal friends. A number of persons in direct touch with him form the first narrow circle of his supporters. It steadily widens through the transmission of opinion from person to person, until an impressive community has been formed, commanding attention and continually attracting new members. It has begun by bringing in those who are attracted by their own independent judgement, and it then goes on to attract the great mass of the uncritical.

There are classic examples of this in the history of literature. The painter Benjamin Robert Haydon introduced Keats to the works of Wordsworth. That is a typical case. Browning discovered Shelley for himself, a less usual happening; he was so proud of it—not without reason—that he celebrated the event with fine similes in his poems. At times the fame of a literary work is carried far and wide on the waves of an ethical, social, or political movement, of which the work may become to some extent the symbol.

But any close observation of art in past and present quickly reveals that the process of sociological taste-forma-

---

[1] See in this connexion H. F. Schulz, *Das Schicksal der Bücher*, Berlin, 1952, pp. 103 ff.

tion is not so much like the automatic spread of waves when a stone is thrown into the water as these examples might suggest. It is not so simple as that; conditions are no longer so primitive.

The relation of the creative artist to current taste. The importance of being comprehended

To begin with, a not unimportant part is played in the creation of a work of art by the existing taste. This does not mean, of course, that art is a commodity deliberately produced to suit the public taste. It has been shown above how, in this precise respect, conditions have changed not a little in the past century. Churchyard, a contemporary of Shakespeare, wrote in a dedication, with cynical frankness, that he took the fish as his exemplar—he swam with the stream: another case in point is Dryden who admitted quite openly that what he was really concerned about was to win the contemporary public for himself, and if that public was determined to have a rather low kind of comedy or satire, then there was nothing he could do save adapt himself ('I will force my genius to obey it')—this idea has pretty well vanished in recent times. In practice, it is true, things do not look quite so rosy. Arnold Bennett, one of the most successful novelists of the recent past, even imagined that he had exposed a conventional lie by openly and energetically contending that the writer had a right to make concessions to public taste. He wrote:

> The truth is that an artist who demands appreciation from the public on his own terms, and on none but his own terms, is either a god or a conceited and impractical fool. And he is somewhat more likely to be the latter than the former. He wants too much. There are two sides to every bargain, including the artistic. The most fertile and the most powerful artists are the readiest to recognise this, because their sense of proportion, which is the sense of order, is well developed. The lack of the sense of proportion is the mark of the *petit maître*. The sagacious artist, while respecting himself, will respect the idiosyncrasies of the public. To do both simultaneously is quite possible.

Arnold Bennett went on to quote as example sexual problems, of which the British public could not stomach the sort of treatment they receive on the Continent. The example was well chosen, though it is now largely out of date in Britain; it does show how certain taboos may fetter artistic individuality. He mentions Shakespeare and Samuel Richardson as great artists who were guided by what the public likes. He might with much better reason have adduced Byron, who, for all his show of independence, never lost sight of his public. Indeed he often made a very timid retreat. When, to quote but a single instance, his pious compatriots took exception to the heresies contained in *Cain* he sought to appease them by declaring that it was not he but his characters who uttered these opinions. It was only after he had fully severed himself from his country, and in the meantime had become sufficiently famous to be able to count on readers all over the world, that he was completely frank in his utterances. Indeed he now actually began to see certain advantages in writing 'against the public'. Certainly these writers made concessions. But the essential question is whether a man sacrifices his individuality. If he does that he simply has not the qualities that make a great artist. These will always involve a certain measure of independence that cannot be influenced.

Arnold Bennett recommends the writer to catch the public eye by a happy, carefully calculated throw, and then to try to draw it along his own path. This last method, applied in a different direction, is often used with success. Artists who have begun in some definite tradition which has helped to win favour for their work gain in this way a charter, within limits, for the pursuit of new paths, along which they come to the full development of their peculiar gift. They have secured a public, and their public remains faithful to them. This was plainly shown in the inquiry of the Leipziger Buchhändler-Börsenverein: one-third of the purchasers gave as their reason for buying the fact that they knew the author's other works.

It is only rarely, of course, that all this is planned by the artist as Arnold Bennett recommends. What happens is usually entirely uncalculated and more or less unconscious; it corresponds to the natural course of human development, which usually adjusts itself in some measure to the environment and is strongly influenced by exemplars.

The attempt to lead the public into fresh fields does not always succeed easily or without sacrifice. The sacrifice was too much for a certain painter of marshland: he was endlessly painting meadows with high skies and admirable roan cattle with little anatomical faults. They had brought him fame, and then he was for ever sighing for a chance to attack other problems. He would have attacked them, if only the public had not continued always to demand from him nothing but meadows with high skies and the admirable roan cattle and the little anatomical faults.[1]

In any case, the situation of a gifted artist who neither consciously nor unconsciously reveals kinship with the dominant taste is not a comfortable one. Many such artists are foredoomed to failure. For tradition is strong and attracts those artists who more or less share it or can follow it. But of those who in their hearts want to go other ways, most will find no opportunity of expressing themselves, or will soon be silenced.

It may be objected that great talent always reveals itself even in unfamiliar forms, and that it is rarely unaccompanied by strong will, which refuses to be discouraged and silenced by failure. But those who argue thus have learnt little from the history of literature or of art. Artistic creation is not the outcome of calculated consideration but the crystallisation of an emotional experience. Such crystallisation, however, is

---

[1] Conversely the artist in his creative work may come under the influence of a current—the formation of the current will be discussed later—which carries him off his natural balance by destroying his confidence and making him so afraid of just repeating himself that he feels driven into continual advance, with the result that instead of making unconscious progress he goads himself into efforts that make him more and more dependent on the outer world, and his best talents atrophy.

often dependent on external circumstances. Artists are sensitive, and, like the gods, they live on incense. No incense, no gods. Recognition gives wings to the artist, neglect and non-recognition may easily prevent high flights. Thus the real tragedy of ill-success lies not in the fact that the creative artist fails to enjoy the effect of his creation, but in the premature crippling of his hands. For many men the first condition of self-confidence is the confidence of others.

It is also impossible to uphold the objection that creative art is an inescapable necessity for the true artist himself. Not every athlete runs the race. Moreover, in all creation there is a moment when the picture of the work of art is seen in the mental vision of the artist. For the artist himself his problem is then three-quarters solved, and there is a danger that at that moment the process ends, if no incentive exists or comes, to induce him to undertake the work, often laborious, of detailed execution. This incentive lies in the thought of the public. Goethe well says:

> What were I without thee,
> O my friend the public?
> All my impressions monologues,
> Silent all my joys!

Where material circumstances do not come into question, the public may often be represented by a single person. A good example of this is the poet Annette von Droste Hülshoff (1797–1848). No one will deny her power and originality of talent. Seen in relation to the background of the poetic achievements of her time, her independence seems again and again to be incredible. And yet, on what chances her creative work depended! For years the source of her work seems as if it had dried up. If she had not found the one individual she cared for and who entirely understood her, what would have become of her art? She says in a letter that without him she would 'recite her poetry to herself'—that is to say, would have written nothing down.

But here we have only a striking example of something

that is to be found in one form or another in all poetic or artistic creation. Think how the art even of a Goethe was roused into fresh life by the intercourse with someone whom he felt to be congenial. Many artists, however, are not so easily contented as Droste, not satisfied to have just one follower. Arnold Bennett points out how even those who affect to despise the crowd usually suffer severely from lack of sympathy. This was true, for instance, of Shelley. Certainly there was never a poet of independent spirit so completely dominated by the urge of his mission as Shelley, as he pursued his solitary path; and yet, how that great lyric poet suffered under the lack of recognition! The deep oppression that burdened him, the gloom that has left its traces on many of his works, would, in the opinion of many who were intimate with him, have been swept away by a single success with the public. 'Nothing is more difficult and unwelcome as to write without a confidence of finding readers.' So he once sighed in a letter to his friend Peacock (*Letters*, ed. Ingpen, II, 848). And he was a man of independent means.

If the external circumstances of an artist's existence are also against him, his whole production is only too likely to collapse. Artistic creation is, as has already been shown, not necessarily something that erupts, forcing its way out with elemental violence. Arnold Bennett quotes a significant passage on this point from a letter of George Meredith's to a friend. Meredith writes that he has hung up his poetry on a nail: 'And in truth, being a servant of the public, I must wait till my master commands before I take seriously to singing.' This, though coloured, perhaps, by bitterness, contains a kernel of truth. But external circumstances deny to artistic gifts in many cases the very beginnings of productive achievement. Gray was not so far from the truth in his *Elegy* when he philosophised about the 'mute inglorious Miltons' resting in the country churchyard. But mute poets do not lie only in the village churchyards. In the absence of the conditions for artistic achievement, in the absence of interest and sympathy and understanding, there is no achievement.

In every field of art these things are usually entirely mis-understood. It is found that at a particular period or in a particular region there was a lack of talents, and it is imagined that it is a question, so to speak, of a good or bad vintage. A famous writer on the history of art, Pinder, imagined that he had discovered the principal key to the understanding of the history of art in the idea of the homo-geneity of the members of 'generations'; he even finds that 'Nature grants rhythmical pauses for breath between the creation of outstanding spirits', and speaks of 'Nature's throws'. Wonderful interpretations of the development of the soul of a people play a part in other explanations. Thus, for instance, the lack of great achievements in English drama in the nineteenth century is explained by Mary Suddard as due to a (mythical) 'lack of cohesion in the creative spirit'; or a highly reputed art critic, Meyer-Gräfe, points out that in the seventeenth century 'the constellation of the German intellect' was such that it turned away from the fine arts to music. That is pure mysticism. What should be inquired into is the reason why there was a lack of opportunity for the emergence of talents. For where men are, there are talents.

Formation of groups and schools

But the general appearance of similar characteristic features in individual works of art which we describe as a definite trend of taste is due, among other reasons, especially to some particular work having success, and attracting the attention of those who take pleasure in creative work. It calls into play the subconscious imitation that is one of the most powerful forces in this as in all other fields of social life. 'Nothing succeeds like success.' It is not a question here of conscious processes, as in the cases which Arnold Bennett has in mind. What happens is that it is in the nature of things for art to inspire art. This tendency is assisted by the fact that no class of men is so drawn as the artist type to associate with kindred souls. Solitude has been described as the artist's Muse, but with only limited justification.

But even the most comprehending environment is not so stimulating for the artist as his fellow-worker. From him he will accept criticism which from the most sympathetic layman is apt to leave a sting. Only the recognition of those who are themselves gifted really counts in his opinion, and the observation of others' achievement stimulates him to emulation. Only in seeing another's full growth does he himself grow to full proportions.

Thus we may follow at all times this formation of groups of artists, so infinitely important to the creation of art. It confirms the truth of the generalisation that in the spiritual as in the material field only diamond can cut diamond. Where these groups cannot be formed, artistic creation is made more difficult. Thus the growth of the Elizabethan drama was especially favoured by the fact that all talents congregated in London and only there, and one could climb on the shoulders of another; whereas in the Germany of that time men of talent lived in isolation, with no mutual influencing to awake their best powers.

In that way it is particularly easy for a common foundation, a school, to come into existence. It is true, of course, that, especially in more modern times, personal intercourse of this sort is not necessary. Influence may be impersonal. The process is then similar, but at times it is, perhaps, more strongly influenced by the fact of outward success.

VI

MEANS OF SELECTION

The importance of the selecting authorities
BUT while it is thus clear how certain influences are active
at the very birth of a work, pushing it, so to speak, in a
particular direction, this is so in an altogether different
degree with the selective forces to which it is exposed after
birth; for of late the production of a literary work has been
little more than coming to birth. Its fate still depends on
many external factors. To the reader of our histories of
literature it might well seem as if the works with which they
deal automatically gained the eye and the ear of the public,
as if they took the place in public opinion that was due to
them as a matter of course, much as the heir ascends the
throne. But the cases in which a man has awakened one
morning like Lord Byron to find himself famous are few and
far between. The mere admission for the first time past the
guards at the entrance to the temple of literary fame is
dependent on definite conditions. Such guards are the
theatrical directors and the publishers. These persons are
largely influenced in their judgement by the consideration of
the public, but there is, nevertheless, a good proportion of
the force of destiny in their personal decisions.

Historically regarded, the publisher begins to play a part
at the stage at which the patron disappears, in the eighteenth
century. There is no uncertainty about this among the poets.

Thus Alexander Pope, when writing to Wycherley on 20 May 1709, sounds a mocking note at the expense of Jacob Tonson the celebrated publisher and editor of an authoritative anthology. Jacob, he declares, creates poets in the same way as kings sometimes created knights. Another publisher, Dodsley, was later to exercise similar privileged powers and so become the target of Richard Graves's witty verses

> 'In vain the poets from their mine
> Extract the shining mass,
> Till Dodsley's Mint has stamped the coin
> And bids the sterling pass.'

And indeed such publishing firms gradually become a source of authority. Who would conceive the English literature of that century without a Dodsley, or the German of the following century without a Cotta? Such publishing firms gradually become a sort of authority. Once Cotta had succeeded in assembling a number of the most eminent 'classic' writers in his publications it became for decades a sort of title to immortality to be published by him, and poets who were striving towards the peaks were never content unless they had the classic griffins of that firm on their title-page. Many modern firms are purely commercial concerns, and the personal taste of their head, such as it may be, takes shelter behind the critical verdict of his anonymous 'reader', male or female, but publishers with pronounced views of their own still exert real influence over the taste of the day. Past successes have brought these latter firms into the confidence of the public, which in taking new works from them feels a certain guarantee of their literary merit. The success of these works is not, of course, thereby assured, but the appearance of a work in the lists of one of these publishers at least carries the suggestion that an aesthetic authority has pronounced in its favour, so that it is sure to arouse favourable expectation.

Theatre managers have, of course, still greater influence; it is enough to mention the example of Otto Brahm to make plain how greatly an individual may help to determine the general trend of taste by his choice. It is also particularly instructive to observe how often the fate of an original work, which has found imitators and created a school, has depended on the taste of a particular publisher or theatre lessee.

Authors who subsequently became famous have knocked in vain on door after door. What would have happened if they had accepted refusal and given up! One of the earliest examples of this sort is Ben Jonson's *Every Man in his Humour*. Tradition said in the eighteenth century that it had been actually rejected when the manuscript came into Shakespeare's hands, and that Shakespeare accepted it for performance in his own theatre. Its influence was as great as that of almost any work of the period. The number of such stories from later centuries is legion. They all show how much has depended on the persistence of the author and what an important part external circumstances have played in his life.

For such authorities as these have, of course, their less admirable side. Even apart from the arbitrariness and chanciness of their method, they offer no adequate guarantee that a work will ever reach the stage of actual consideration. As a rule the theatre manager is much too busy to be able to cope with the flood of manuscripts submitted to him. And as a rule the part played by the *Dramaturg*[1] is too insignificant—how instructive a monograph on this subject would be! The result is a natural reluctance to make experiments and a tendency of the theatres in the smaller towns to make no effort at discoveries of their own and to rely on works that appear to have succeeded at one of the few great theatres. This tendency is reinforced by the dangerous dependence on

[1] The English theatre knows no exact equivalent to the German Dramaturg. The Dramaturg's function is not only to select plays, but also very frequently to rewrite them. In Germany where repertory was well established and universal long before it became established in England, and where a more flexible relationship existed between actor and producer on the one hand and the play on the other, this functionary was often very useful.

theatrical publishers. Thus the smaller towns lose, as a rule, all influence in this field.

As regards getting published, one fact has been observable since at least the eighteenth century—the fortunate situation of anyone who is in personal touch with writers who are well known and have their public and a certain prestige with the publishers. Their recommendation may carry sufficient weight to smooth away the main difficulties for the new-comer. Thus it is almost a rule that the beginner's work does not pass direct from him to the appropriate authority, but takes the indirect and often difficult course past the desk of an artist of repute.

This method has its imperfections. In comparison with it, the method of scientific achievement seems almost ideal. The recognition of the defects of the method has led to many attempts at reform. Prizes have been instituted and com-mittees formed with the aid of which it has been hoped to discover hitherto unrevealed treasures. And indeed it is im-possible to deny that institutions such as the Pulitzer Prize which has been awarded by Columbia University in New York since 1917, or the Goncourt Prize for Literature, awarded since 1902, exercise a certain influence. In the same way the Nobel Prize for Literature, which has been awarded by the Academy of Stockholm since 1901 and which was once capable of being a world sensation even to-day can cause the name of an unknown person to be on everybody's lips overnight. However, it has, thanks to certain rather curious decisions, disputed by the international *cognoscenti*, lost the authority which it once enjoyed. Nevertheless we must still recognise a force here which contributes powerfully to the formation of taste.

Use of means of propaganda
The layman's conception of the course which the work of art follows, so to speak, of its own accord, also takes no account of the fact that the course has long been determined by all sorts of material considerations. In many respects,

though certainly not in all, there is a parallel here with the development in commercial life, in which consumer and producer have long been separated by many intermediate elements which exercise extraordinary influence on both sides.

There is an English example of this that, to anyone who regards creative intellectual work as more or less entirely dependent on intellectual causes, must seem almost insultingly profane. The three-volume novel of Thackeray's and Dickens's day was so universally the accepted form that Charlotte Brontë's first novel, *The Professor*, was at first rejected everywhere, mainly because it was produced in a single volume. Suddenly, at the beginning of the 'nineties, this form died out. The reason for this was that the great lending libraries declared that they would no longer accept it. This happened in 1894. In that year 184 three-volume novels were published; in 1897 only four.

The change may have been long in preparation owing to various circumstances, but the quick death of the old form was due entirely to material causes. Here is an instance, therefore, of the influencing of creative work. But those who look around them with their eyes open will not fail to perceive that the spread of taste in regard to works of art may be determined not only by the conflict of ideas but by a competition of very concrete elements of power. The birth of the publishing trade, and of the trade in works of art, introduced a struggle for the public. The history of the development of publishing methods would be one of the most interesting, though not the most edifying, chapters in a history of literary taste. Advertising in matters of art is generally regarded as a modern acquisition, but this is an over-estimate of the idealism of past generations. It is now nothing new for an author to do his best to pave the way for his works. There is plenty of evidence in existence for this, at any rate since the middle of the eighteenth century. One of the first of the famous men of modern literature to recognise the necessity of advertisement in this world that is so

slow of perception was the great Cervantes. Fearing, perhaps
not without reason, that the first part of *Don Quixote* would
not meet with the recognition it deserved, he had a small
pamphlet published which affected to criticise the book and
hinted that it contained all sorts of dangerous satires on
highly placed personages. This well-thrown snowball
brought down upon the book a veritable avalanche of
criticisms and polemics. Another active collaborator with his
publisher was the author of *Tristram Shandy* and the *Sentimental Journey*: he actually dictated to his mistress letters in
which she drew the attention of her acquaintances in London
to the amazing new book by the hitherto unknown clergyman Laurence Sterne.

The close professional relationship between author and
journalist, at times an actual personal union, facilitates the
process of influencing by roundabout methods. In such
matters both great and lesser artists have everywhere and at
all times been none too scrupulous. At one time, in the
'forties, Levin Schücking published an article on Franz
Dingelstedt, and shortly afterwards Dingelstedt published
one on Schücking. This aroused the wrath of the meti-
culously honest Freiligrath, and he sent a strong letter to his
friend Schücking in which he declared that apparently a
joint-stock company had been formed; but this was but a
rather innocent example of the mutual admiration societies
of which there have been many more striking instances in the
history of literature. One of Scribe's comedies *La Camara-
derie* (1837) made very witty fun of this practice. A familiar
one is the work done by the friends of Dante Gabriel Rossetti,
the father of the Pre-Raphaelite Movement, when his long-
withheld poems, some of them rescued from his wife's grave,
were at last published: Rossetti's circle had taken care to
get into their hands the reviewing of the poems for the
principal newspapers. This seems to have been the thing
that most contributed to rousing George Buchanan to launch
against Rossetti the wild and bitter assault of his *Fleshly
School* pamphlet, which was the first of the attacks that

destroyed for ever the mental balance of the sensitive Rossetti. Friendly services of that sort are recorded on every page of the history of literature; seldom have they had such tragic results.

Of almost venerable antiquity are the efforts in theatrical life, very naturally called forth by the circumstances of production, to encourage the public to overcome its shyness in expressing sympathy with the play put before it. In the English theatre of the eighteenth century the claque, for instance, was an entirely ordinary feature, and Fielding gives a vivid description of the way the system could lead, if the public refused to be drummed into applause, to an uproar amid which timid lady members of the audience fled in terror. Even the foremost writers of that day clearly saw nothing reprehensible in such activities. The claque was elaborately organised for the successful production of Voltaire's *Orestes* (1750), and at the first performance of *She Stoops to Conquer* (15 March 1773) the 'organisation of the public' was so perfect that success was assured. A body of sturdy fellows, most of them Scots, chosen by the size of their hands and of their voices, were adroitly distributed among the audience. Dr Johnson—so Richard Cumberland relates[1]—was sitting in one of the boxes, and the leader of this claque, a man whose laugh was so stentorian that he could overbear alone the shouts of a full house, was instructed to keep his eye on Dr Johnson; at the doctor's nod he was to give out his irresistible horse-laugh. Yet, as a rule, Dr Johnson was an admirer of sayings of the utmost gravity.

The propaganda of later times was less barefaced but not less effectual. Many new and more refined devices were discovered, but their effectiveness is patent. The art of working upon the public mind has been made the subject of careful study, and the results have proved their value in all sorts of ways.

There is, of course, nothing to object to in advertisement that aims, as it is entitled to, at reaching as many ears as possible; it is, indeed, a mistake to do without it. But all sorts of

[1] *Memoirs*, Vol. 1, pp. 367–8.

dubious practices and dodges make their appearance at times. There are art dealers who openly boast of having made a particular artist famous, and there are publishers with a similar ambition, who scheme to draw writers, critics, and especially newspapers within the sphere of their mostly very material interests and cleverly make use of them. And it is no longer unusual for an influential newspaper to open its columns only to praise of a writer who enjoys its favour, and to suppress everything that is said against him.

The public is inclined to regard these things as trivial human failings and to hold that it is the muse and not the publisher that makes the poet, and that publicity does not make bad work good. There is something in this, of course, and publicity by no means always brings success. A few years before 1914 an experiment on an almost Napoleonic scale was made in Germany with the 'Ganter Letters'. A small fortune was sunk in reaching many thousands of cultured people one morning with an anonymous letter directing their attention by means of distributing insinuations, concerning all manner of highly personal matters, to a novel that had just appeared. But apart from the worthlessness of the novel, the campaign was fatuous and a complete failure. But the mere fact that it was attempted is significant.

Many writers try to find publishers who will 'do something' for their books; and, after all, they know what they are about. For publicity cannot make a Goethe out of a nobody; but— a fact the publicity rarely realises—it can nevertheless do a great deal to smooth the way for particular trends in taste, heightening their importance in the eyes of the uncritical, and so blocking the path for others.

Many and varied expedients can, of course, be made to serve such ends. It is not always easy to ascertain after the event how far certain stages on the path to Parnassus have been paid for, so to speak, with false coins. Sometimes there are irreproachable factors working in the same direction. Samuel Rogers, the author of the *Pleasures of Memory* (1792), was a rich man with great influence in social and literary life, popular and, on the other hand, feared for his sharp tongue; these conditions were not without importance in determining his literary standing during his life. His works have not earned lasting fame. But this is poor consolation for those whom he threw into the shade while he lived.

In this field of public life things happen in the same way as in other fields. Facile phrases about the good making its way. in the end may comfort many an unrecognised man of talent, but they fall wide of the truth. They recall the saying that where the need is greatest God's help is nearest—a useful source, perhaps, of encouragement in desperate situations, but of very doubtful logical validity in spite of all the touching instances recorded in old lesson-books. Such faith will help the creative artist, but the literary or sociological observer who holds unreservedly to it is lacking in the critical faculty. To the belief that the good wins through, the critic can only offer the sceptical reply that that which wins through will thereafter be regarded as good.

Importance of literary criticism
The control of visas for the travellers to Parnassus is in the hands of the literary critic. He is usually regarded as the main driving force in the history of taste. In the course of the history of literary criticism, as Professor Saintsbury first pointed out, and as in more recent times René Wellek has demonstrated in classical form, critics with discrimination have not seldom exercised a certain influence over development; most of these, it is true, were men who had themselves engaged in some sort of creative activity.[1] The judgement, however carefully balanced, of a single critic, however famous, has not usually been of great moment. There are many cases, indeed, in which a consensus of praise of a novel or poem was of no decisive effect if it had not the support of the other forces already mentioned. The inquiry made by the Leipziger Buchhändler-Börsenverein revealed 391 cases in which a book had been bought on the recommendation of a friend, and only

[1] For instance, Addison, Diderot, or Lessing.

195 purchases due entirely to a review. The most influential critics are still those who regularly write for a particular newspaper or periodical and who have succeeded in gaining the confidence and respect of their readers. In this regard the organs which have a special association with their subscribers have an advantage. In these cases, as under more primitive circumstances, a personal relationship is then set up between critic and reader. The reader ascertains the critic's taste and tendency, and thereafter trusts more or less to his guidance.

This guidance becomes still more important in the case of fine-art periodicals which offer not only criticism but examples, so that the critic is to some extent publisher as well. The publisher of such periodicals—and among them we must reckon certain publishers' and book societies' organs—have a good deal of influence over the development of taste. Sometimes in these cases the result is the formation of regular communities, whose members are more or less in agreement with one another not only in their taste but in their political, social, and religious views. These cases are particularly interesting, because they show how easily aesthetic judgements are shared by particular social groups.

It would be worth while to throw closer and more penetrating light on the interesting sociological conditions existing in these cases. Work on the history of such groups of readers or communities, for instance, as gathered in Germany in the past round the 'Gartenlaube', and later the 'Rundschau', the 'Neue Rundschau', the 'Kunstwart', 'Türmer', 'Hochland', 'Welt und Wort', and so on, might lead to important conclusions concerning the history of taste, that is to say, concerning the establishment of the contemporary existence of various strata of taste and their influence on each other—conclusions by means of which the ultimate differences in culture in general would finally be grasped. In this way light would simultaneously be thrown on the peculiar tacit constitutional relationship between publisher and public, which to some extent binds the former to a certain extent to the will of the latter. This connexion was a good deal closer in the past. We need only refer to a single case, namely, Thackeray's action while Editor of the *Cornhill Magazine* in the matter of Elizabeth Barrett Browning's poem 'Lord Walter's Wife'. Thackeray took months to come to a decision, and ultimately returned the poem to its author on the grounds that his sensitive readers would be outraged by the high degree of unlawful passion felt by a man for a woman. What is significant in this case is the strict responsibility which an editor assumed on behalf of his readers. To us it appears to savour somewhat of what the English would call Mrs Grundy and the Germans 'Biedermeierlich'. Thus in this relationship, too, there have been important changes.

The causes underlying these changes are discernible also in the changed standpoint of the critic. The history of past centuries shows us many generations of critics whose criteria were no more than rules which they had drawn from classic art or the art of the past, and who were accordingly entirely without comprehension of anything that was new. In the period of classicism literature has the appearance of a garden in which countless gardeners are busy trimming the seedlings of art. Their successors are, so to speak, the sterile brains that made life bitter for many an artist who had something of importance to say to the world—artists of the calibre of a Keats or a Hebbal. The nineteenth century in Germany, however, experienced a complete change in these things in its last decades. There was no more of the state of things that had been almost universal, when the rising artist regarded the critic as his sworn enemy, whose right to exist he never tired of contesting in private talk by means of every paradox of which an artist's thinking is capable.

The battle-cry 'Kill him, he's a critic!' has long lost its popularity. The critic takes much more trouble than in the past to do justice to the artist's individuality, to enter into his ideas, to assess the value of his aims. He no longer pronounces verdicts as a judge according to the rigid formulas of an obsolete code, but serves as an expert interpreter, smoothing away difficulties in the way of comprehension where necessary.

Much excellent work has been done in this way. Almost un-
noticed, however, some critics, particularly, so far as literature is concerned, the theatrical critics of the great cities, have
completely changed their attitude, placing themselves now
unconditionally in the service of the artist. This development,
paralleled in past centuries in periods during which art thrust
a barrier between itself and public taste, is not yet of very
long standing in Germany. Not until the death of the Berlin
theatrical producer Otto Brahm (1912) who pioneered for
Ibsen and Hauptmann was the point made in Berlin obitu-
aries, almost by way of praise, that he was the father of a
generation of critics who were not afraid to write against the
public. That has had no little influence over art life.

This is a group-formation of the most important sort, and
one that has existed in similar form in the past, but an astonishing one in face of all that has gone before. In Germany in
the past, and often to this day, theatrical criticism in the
small towns has not been a profession but has been in the
hands of writers or educated laymen. The critic felt himself
to be at most *primus inter pares* in the auditorium. He was the
representative of the educated public, the mouthpiece of its
claims; at all events, he claimed that status. E. T. A. Hoffmann, for instance, in a letter from Bamberg gave this reply
to an invitation to act as music critic for a Bamberg review:

'In so far as I express a personal opinion in that article, I
shall hold loyally and conscientiously to the judgement of the
public, and so shall myself be the only organ of public
opinion.'

That part is no longer played by the critic. In the life of
art a process has taken place resembling that which took
place in religion when the priest thrust himself between God
and the believers. Sometimes one has the impression that
God is there only for the priest; in any case, he floats high
above the common crowd of the laity. At the beginning of
the century Berlin witnessed the curious spectacle in which a
critic like Alfred Kerr, who had no hesitation in regarding his
own function as superior to that of a mere dramatist, actually

endeavoured to argue the public out of any liking for the kind of dramatic art of which he disapproved. Indeed he almost tried to forbid them to take any pleasure in it. One of the victims of this propaganda, namely, Hermann Sudermann, vainly sought to defend himself by his articles on the 'Brutalising of Berlin theatrical criticism'. Whether the journalistic victory of this critic of dramatic art in Germany served on balance the interest of the latter may well be doubted; that such a victory was possible is enough to show us that a radical change had taken place in the relations between the public and the critic. Such a view as the famous one of Heinrich Laube that the true connoisseurs sit in the gallery seems entirely incomprehensible. In dramatic criticism expressions have been coined, such as 'the play had an external success' or even 'the play succeeded with the public', expressions that speak volumes. The public is more or less put under the control of a trustee.

This type of judgement is to be found even more crudely expressed in the realm of the fine arts. Here the expert's sense of omniscience has no bounds at all. In 1929 the University of Erlangen decided on the erection of a war memorial of its own choice. The *Münchener Neueste Nachrichten*, the most widely circulated newspaper in Bavaria, on 29 July denounced this decision of a body 'without authority in questions of art'. Yet, why should not highly cultured laymen be credited with judgement in questions of art?

Still, the position is not very different in the other arts. Nothing shows this more clearly than the fact that many newspapers have almost ceased to report the attitude of the public at first performances. This has been noticeable in the 'leading' criticisms in Berlin since some years before 1914. The reception accorded to a play scarcely matters. There are theatres such as that of Louise Dumont at Düsseldorf in which this situation has, so to speak, become law, applause and expressions of disapproval being alike done away with. The theatre thus deals, as it were, with Messieurs the Critics direct. The right of aesthetic pronouncement is regarded as withdrawn from the public and placed in the hands of the all-powerful critic. The critic becomes a sort of aesthetic inspecting authority in relation to the public.

This development has a triple root—the change in the position of art and artist in life discussed in Chapter III; the divisions and resulting impotence of the public, also sketched above, and finally the historic reasons that go back to the literary revolution of naturalism. The hard struggle that naturalism had to carry on against the backwardness of a public that had been far from being backward only in the field of art ended with a complete defeat of the public. But any belated recognition was bound to furnish fresh food for the dogma that to-day appears to be beyond all questioning, that the public is simply not in a position to comprehend the true artist when he appears. Was this not the experience of Wagner in music, of Hebbel in literature, of Böcklin in painting? These examples were for many years in the mouths of everybody the moment the question of the relationship between art and public cropped up.

It had been completely forgotten how differently things had been regarded but a few generations earlier. Even Grillparzer, for instance, held that the public was, if not a judge learned in the law, at all events a jury, pronouncing 'guilty' or 'not guilty' according to sound common sense and natural feeling. For the dramatist the public was therefore the best authority. A play that failed with the public could not be a good play. The fault was bound to lie with the play. Similarly the young Schiller had contended that it was not the public that pulled art down: art degenerated always through the artists (Fritz Strich). Even so independent a critic as Shelley, who on occasion expressed his disrespect for contemporary criticism clearly enough, wrote in the preface to one of his principal works, *The Revolt of Islam,* the following strangely submissive-sounding words: 'Should the Public judge that my composition is worthless, I shall indeed bow before the tribunal from which Milton received his crown of immortality.' The position in Germany is no different. Now it is certainly true that an entirely novel development in taste does not make its way easily at first; but it would be a serious distortion of the facts of the past to say that all really great artists have at first met with incomprehension. It would be overlooking the furore created by Goethe's *Werther*, the popularity of Shakespeare in his own day, and the idolisation of Byron from the very outset. It is possible to be understood from the first and yet to be a great artist. On the other hand, to fail to please is no proof of importance.

Yet, with an extraordinary exaggeration, the theory of the incomprehension of the crowd is carried to the length of that paradox of which Nietzsche was so fond—'They are clapping: what nonsense have I been talking?' In other words, the main criterion for art seemed to be its entire departure from earlier taste. For a long time the impression, certainly mistaken, existed that a work found favour with the critics only if it ran full tilt against those postulates which earlier generations had regarded as of the very essence of dramatic form. Consider, for instance, how contemptuously the metropolitan critics used to write of Eugène Brieux's *Red Robe* (1900) with its magnificent qualities as pure drama. Or the attitude of the critics to Karl Schönherr's *Glaube und Heimat* (1910). This was a play with really agonising inner conflicts, a drama of deep human content. Millions of Germans were in a position to enter with the deepest sympathy into the spiritual struggles it represented. The play thus succeeded everywhere. But the critics of the capital cities, who found such virtues in so many brothel dramas, treated it with lofty contempt as a 'thriller'. How many chances of the birth of a dramatic art of permanent value to the German nation were thus thrown away! And, on the other hand, on how few of those on whose work and will the social progress of their people really depended did Wedekind, for instance, the dramatist who at about the same time was being praised to the skies by the high priests of 'pure literature', have any intellectual influence—Wedekind, whom current historians of literature continue to take so seriously as an outstanding contemporary! Their number is infinitesimal in comparison with the 'literary' reputation of his works. What it all comes to is a ceaseless hunt in packs for new means of expression in art, in the course of which the spiritual values which the layman demands from art are lost sight of altogether.

This, in fact, is where the public and the art critics part company. The public—in so far as it has not lost all aesthetic orientation and fallen into the state described by Hans Andersen in the story of the king's new clothes—is out to enjoy a work of art, but the art critic, using the term in its widest sense, is out to discover, as a Berlin critic once put it, a new 'art-will'. His complaint of the public is that it is too ready to rest sleepily content with old forms. But the public can retort that the critic is always chasing the day after to-morrow. It may also be asked whether a specialism does not here come into existence that, in its unceasing introspection, inevitably loses touch with sound common sense.

Nobody will deny that the authorities here under discussion possess a high degree of expertise. Often, too, as shown above, there have been periods in the history of literature in which the production of artistic achievements has been made possible by the sounding-board of a small and relatively limited circle of connoisseurs. But never in such cases has art been regarded as something that, as it were, is outside life. There is a sort of parallel to this in law. The world has long realised that the professional jurist easily falls into a formalistic ossification in the conception of legal circumstances. Consequently there has arisen a mistrust that accounts for the institution of the lay magistrate. Most jurists have no love for him. But in the judgement of questions of art a professional connoisseurship has come into existence that has departed still further from sound common sense. The law's *fiat justitia, pereat mundus* may be translated in the field of art by *l'art pour l'art*.

Influences from the fine arts
Now, no one is more inclined than the historian to caution in

questions of the development of taste. He has learned how often in the course of centuries the representatives of an established taste have condemned as mere novelty-mongering and an ephemeral fashion the first appearance of a change that subsequently won general recognition. On the other hand, no one knows better than the historian that there have in fact been periods that have wallowed in unnaturalness and artificiality, and that it must accordingly be useful to discover the sociological reasons for this. This is, of course, a phenomenon that extends far beyond the literary sphere. Often, a matter of fundamental importance to the question of the formation of taste, it has actually drawn its inspiration from the neighbouring sphere of the fine arts. For wherever one group of people is instrumental in shaping the taste in the case of all the different categories of art—and this must never be taken for granted but must be clearly established in every single case—an effort will sooner or later be made to apply the principles underlying one such category to all the rest, insofar as the heterogeneous forms of expression admit of this possibility. Thus a complete transformation of taste in regard to one category of art can be projected on to another and entirely different one. It often happens that one category of art develops a relation of complete dependence upon another. We have spoken already of the way the relationship between literature and the fine arts has gradually been so completely inverted that speech itself bears the traces of the change, in the word 'artist'. This is but one example of many similar phenomena showing the changing influence of the arts on one another in the course of centuries. In the eighteenth century the older landscape painting exercised for a time a controlling influence over nature-writing. Many sceneries have been pictured not from Nature but from Salvator Rosa (1615–1673). Men approach Nature herself with 'Claude glasses', thus declaring themselves conquered by the method of observation of Claude Lorrain (1600–1682). Later, in the romantic period, literature visibly gained the advantage, and now we have to do with a thorough-going impregnation of the fine arts with the spirit of literature. We need only point to the paintings of the romanticists, to the relation of Moritz von Schwind to Mörike, or recall the work of the Pre-Raphaelites, which so largely present painted poems.

In our times we see just the opposite. The deliberate turning away of expressionist painters and their successors from truth to nature, the methodical exaggeration, so closely related to caricature, of particular features with the purpose of expressing what seems to the artist to be the essential idea of the object, have produced parallels in certain dramas, the action of which no longer makes any claim to psychological truth in the old sense, and the characters of which reveal deliberate simplifications and heightenings; the drawings whose primitiveness is a return to the form-language of childhood and of primitive races have a counterpart in shriek-like babbling as a means of expression of feeling, and the so-called 'absolute' painting is reflected in a lyricism in which 'reality either suffers destruction or becomes a cipher in a context transcending all reality' (von Wiese).

The power of the fine arts shows itself most plainly in their relation to the stage. Here expressionism has found a footing in the art of production, and has had its triumphs in the *Stilbühne*, the 'stylised stage'. It would be showing lack of appreciation to pass over the wonderful work done in Germany in the art of the stage since about 1910. The mass of ideas here developed, the spiritual application of new technical expedients, continually compel the observer's admiration.

But what is the price of this? Years ago *Hamlet* was played in Vienna between black walls, on a red floor, which the audience was required to take as the churchyard, and across which the characters moved in unlovely caricatures of clothing in monotonous bright colour; we were told that this represented not reality but the picture of reality formed in Hamlet's distraught mind (H. Richter). *Tartuffe* was played in Berlin by cigarette-smokers in soft collars; *Much Ado About Nothing* in Munich with Hero and Beatrice in the peasant costume of the mountain country of Upper Bavaria but with a red and green wig—and we imagined that we had seen this doctrine carried to its culmination. Somewhere else *The Merchant of Venice* was given with the natural Venetian background replaced by an 'ideal local colour', in which the 'fundamentals of the Venetian art style' were discreetly suggested: a large section of the public shook their heads, while most of the critics welcomed the performance with esoteric understanding, not to say with veneration. A production of a Shakespeare play in Upper Bavarian costume is suggestive of the more or less witty self-parodies one used to witness in intimate artists' gatherings at which the conscientious service of the public was replaced by a more light-hearted attitude. But naturally nobody dreamed of parodying in earnest. In this field, as in others, the law was observed that when the given problems are solved others are attacked, unless external circumstances compel a repetition of the old ones.

Continual experimenting with new means of expression leads in the end to caricature, unconscious or deliberate. The most astonishing thing about all this is the helpless passivity of the public which is in evidence from the very beginning of the movement. When in 1921 in the state-owned Schauspielhaus in Berlin Leopold Jessner simply transformed the stage into a set of stairs to the height of an ordinary room, let Richard III call for a horse from such a set of stairs, and Desdemona open her bed upon it, he may well have met with a surprised smile. People may have wondered at the fact that the Expressionist urge towards simplicity, a simplicity that avoided anything that smacked of the theatrical, should—of all things—find its ideal expression in a bare set of stairs. Yet who really took exception or demanded that those responsible should be called to account when a disrespectful piece of bluff was enacted in a state-owned theatre in regard to a matter that had once been regarded as extremely serious, not to say sacred. Indeed the very opposite happened and the more grotesque the effort the more solemn was the official expression on the face of the professional judge. 'This lofty and unassuming simplicity', wrote a leading Berlin critic in 1921 when discussing an *Othello* production of Jessner's (in which Iago appeared on the inevitable stairs in a green shooting jacket, while Othello did so in a flowing yellow gown), 'is meant to indicate that the producer was giving us the kernel and not the mere husk of the matter.'

The later developments of such searching for the kernel of the movement, which to the producers was a licence for every kind of extravagance, are notorious enough. Gradually everything was surpassed that had ever been done to startle and shock the public. In particular symbolism in the scenery achieved an importance which until then had been wholly unsuspected. To what oddities those concerned could on occasion descend is shown by such a production as that of *Lear* at the Stratford Memorial Theatre in 1913. Here in the scene upon the heath where the stage directions prescribe an entrance to a cave the producer had set up a monolith next to that cave. We are told the phallic significance of its shape expresses the obscenities of the Fool in the middle scene.[1] And performances of this sort are possibly given before working-class people!

However, in this trend, which has long since led to a complete dissolution of all tradition, considerations of the public (for which the old problems can in no wise be regarded as put out of date) no longer count.

If, as not seldom happens, this method is applied to plays in which the author had in view a definite local colour or a particular style of costume, the artist serving him makes a forcible entry into his master's realm, and does violence, in regard to the person for whom he is working, to the very respect for artistic individuality which he demands for himself. The development has thus in a certain sense turned full circle and in the conception of art has long returned to the standpoint of the time when, out of lack of respect for the individuality of the creative artist, his works were botched to fit the prevailing fashion in taste. Yet the very persons who in

[1] W. M. Merchant, *Shakespeare and the Artist.*

their histories of literature charge Pope with translating Homer into rococo, or who laugh at a Lady Macbeth in eighteenth-century costume, see no serious inconsistency in such violation of their classics as, for instance, Hamlet's mother in an Eton crop smoking a cigarette.

The fundamental attitude of this trend in art towards the public has been best summarised by one of its advocates (Kandinsky) in the phrase: 'That is beautiful which corresponds to an inner necessity.' This pronouncement shows particularly well the confusion of ideas. The thing he should have said is: An artist should only create that which corresponds to an inner necessity in his own mind. But when that is done, only one of the conditions has been fulfilled for the production of 'the beautiful'. A botcher, an imbecile, or a moral pervert may work as hard as he will under compulsion from within him, and the result will not be beautiful.

Regarded from the point of view of the history of thought, we arrive with this doctrine at the extreme end of the line of development that began with the revolt against the classic in the middle of the eighteenth century. At that time Edward Young, who attained such extraordinary fame with his *Night Thoughts*, taught in his *Conjectures on Original Composition* that the 'rules' that until then had been held sacred were no more than 'crutches' for the lame, and that genius bore its rules within itself. The whole history of the following period is in a certain sense a single process of development of that idea. In the present-day conception of art it has found its *reductio ad absurdum*. The assumptions contained in the word 'genius' have fallen away. The creative artist demands recognition of his taste under all circumstances. A complete dictatorship of taste prescribes that we shall accept the expression of the instincts of anyone who sets out to be an artist, in any form he deigns to choose. The advocates of this view have carried it to the paradoxical claim that the layman must listen in silence in the presence of the majesty of art, and wait till he is spoken to. If he is not spoken to he must silently go away. Thus the proud claims of kings live on, advanced by the artists.

The fact that such pronouncements were not merely academic was shown by the Berlin art exhibitions in which used tram-tickets, bits of the soles of shoes, and the like, were stuck on paintings to heighten the effect. Most of the public then regarded this as contempt of the public.

It is well, however, to realise that the correct explanation of what happened can only be found if here again, instead of speaking about the 'spirit of the age', one is ready to disentangle the antagonistic social forces which have been at work in the last generation. Phenomena such as the Berlin Exhibition are the result of a relentless introversion which alienates the artist from the Real, and of the fact that he lives at the same time in a society of countless competitors where one can become a success only if, following the American device, one 'gets talked about'.

VII

PUBLIC RECOGNITION

The grounds for public recognition: The propaganda value of the new
IT will be contended against the conception here put forward that it is, at bottom, too unspiritual, and that developments are being judged from outward appearances rather than from their intrinsic nature. It will be said that while, in the establishment of a new taste, there do exist all sorts of external influences, these are far from playing a decisive part. If the new taste had no other support, it would scarcely succeed in striking root. If this happens, it must at least be assumed that it has real intrinsic values, that it corresponds to a new and changed general attitude, that, as a newspaper reporter said, 'it forces its way unconsciously from the depth of the soul of the people'.

In reply to this it must first be pointed out that, as has been made clear by what has already been here said, it is impossible simply to identify any particular sociological group with the people as a whole and to regard its feeling as that of the 'soul of the people'. There is also no inheritance in art, and the simple fact of existence establishes no claims in this respect. The fact that a small group adopts a new ideal in art in no way obliges others to follow suit. Its advocates, however, sometimes make excellent progress simply by the appeal to a mystical association with the 'spirit of the age' which they are only themselves helping to create. Those who take such a view of the matter will find food for thought in the circumstance that precisely such a claim is made by the fashion industry. In the very department of life in which we can surely discern the most extravagant antics of subjective mood we stand very solemnly corrected in the memoirs of the Paris designer Poiret (*En habillant l'Époque*), for here we learn that the master's achievement does not lie in the arbitrary invention of new forms, but that this is to be discerned in his ability to adapt himself in advance to women's secret wishes. And yet such modesty does not wholly avoid becoming suspect, for its whole purpose is to endow a designer's work with the added importance which accrues to it from this very fact of being determined by the unspoken desires of the public. It does not differ greatly from the shopkeeper's magic formula —'This is the latest thing'. For nobody wants to be decried as behind the times. The true 'conservative', who values the old because it is old and refuses to consider the new and better, has found his counterpart in the person who thinks he is doing a service when he accepts as a matter of principle every new claim to recognition, thinking he is thus helping youth to secure its rights—an attitude in which the fear of seeming out of date disguises itself as progressiveness. It is difficult, however, to see how such an attitude is compatible with historic culture: did not Shakespeare at the end of his activity fall into the background in face of newer trends which nobody in the world has since valued; did not Rembrandt end by becoming out of date? Was it fine in these cases to side with the new against the older generations?

Yet it must not be overlooked that in the trend towards the new there is an element of youth, for the fact that pretty well all things change is a law that becomes clear to everybody and inability to keep pace with change is a sign of old age. Everybody likes to 'move with the times'. The productive man, in particular, hates to stay for long in mere negation. But if we describe a change as one corresponding to the spirit of the age, in other words as virtually in accordance with law, we stamp those who cannot follow it as grown old.

But why is each change in accordance with law? The proof of it must first be produced. For the time being we see on occasion a thousand forces, which after all are chance forces, at work to produce it. Many of them work by methods that have been taken over from commercial life. But it is not a law even of commercial life that the best establishes itself. We all know cases in which excellent trade products are left high and dry by others that have been launched by successful business methods as more modern. The taste for the new goods has simply been forced on the public, and the older ones must either disappear, accept a secondary place, or copy the business method. Conditions in art life are not as different from this as might seem at a first glance. Here, too, much more can be attained by external means that the reader or listener or spectator dreams. How cleverly things are arranged and introduced which, at a later date, innocent historians of art and literature gravely describe as 'the inevitability of spiritual dynamics' and after profound inquiry into their philosophical foundations explain as the outcome of the 'spirit of the age', when in reality they are the outcome, perhaps, only of the mentality of a particular group that is by no means always obviously identifiable with the people as a whole.

Another consideration is that external means need only accomplish a certain preliminary work, and have, so to speak, only to carry out the launching; once out in the stream of public life, the work proves that it can float if only it has the one indispensable quality of originality.

Literature derives advantage from the fact that in their social gatherings it has for centuries been the favourite subject of educated people's conversation. Anyone who wishes to be *au courant* with his times, and to be able to contribute his share of talk, had to be able to express a definite opinion on any new publication that had excited a certain amount of interest. This is one of the situations in which that rather superficial old saw that birds of a feather flock together most certainly applies. Something comes into being that is a sort of

backbone of taste. This is obviously a very ancient phenomenon, for such a literary 'sensation' was provided as far
back as the twelfth century by the *Historia Regum Britanniae*
from the pen of that clever Celt Geoffrey of Monmouth which
was centuries later to provide the inspiration for the Artus
Epic. A certain Arthur of Beverley bears witness to this. He
says that he had been asked so often whether he had read the
work that he eventually got tired of the question and managed
to acquire the manuscript. Many were later to confess that
they had been moved to read some 'best-seller' by the im-
perious dictates of fashion. Pepys' *Diary* states under date of
16 September 1662 that he had sold his copy of Butler's
Hudibras, which had recently appeared, because the book
seemed to him too simple. Six weeks later, however, he
acquired it afresh because in the meantime the entire world,
the society at the court of Charles II that is to say which set
the tone in those days, had decided that it was a masterpiece
of wit. A hundred years later Richardson, a man of strict
morals, expressed his indignation over the fact that everybody was talking about so frivolous and indecent a book
as Sterne's *Tristram Shandy*. He was deeply distressed by
the fact that nobody can resist the power of fashion and
that people are often compelled to read a worthless book
simply because fashion had made it a favourite topic of
conversation.

Another half-century later Byron, helped by his extreme
good looks, the number of his love affairs, and in particular
the scandal concerning his supposed illicit relations with his
half-sister, Augusta Leigh, had the good fortune to become
the talk of the day, and so was rescued from the profoundest
obscurity and exposed to the blinding glare that is focussed
upon anyone who has become a sensation.

Many similar instances can be found in the history of
literature. In all these cases the purely literary effect is falsi-
fied by a purely social factor. The reader is overwhelmed by
what appears to him to be the *communis opinio* and is, as it
were, silenced by it, so much so that he often makes no

attempt at independent criticism and suddenly sees the work of art in question in a quite different light from that in which he had previously regarded it. 'A book that has achieved a considerable effect can really no longer be criticised at all.' These words were spoken by Goethe on 11 June 1822 to Chancellor von Müller.

Actually a new work need not be sensationally presented to the public at all. For the simple fact that it has a group of supporters attracts widespread support at certain times from some spirits. The thing that grips them is less the work in itself than the circumstance that here is something new, which has proved to the taste of other people. Independent judgement presupposes a sense of quality, a relatively rare possession; consequently people accept the new as the thing that is.

Moreover, we are all more open to influence than we may ourselves be ready to admit. Nobody can resist indefinitely the effect of the thing that is constantly seen or heard. The pacifist Swift makes Gulliver, in the land of the Houyhnhnms, tell of the wars customary in Europe, 'when my Master commanded me Silence . . . My discourse . . . gave him a Disturbance in his mind . . . He thought his Ears being used to such abominable Words, might by Degrees admit them with less Detestation.'[1] That has reference to moral feelings, but the same is true of aesthetic ones. The aesthetic sense is remarkably open to influence. Max Liebermann is said to have exclaimed when a member of a jury at an exhibition: 'Take the picture away, or I shall begin to like it,' and the witticism is not without a deeper meaning. A language of form that at first may seem ugly or affected or unnatural loses its repulsiveness in the long run. Friedrich Gundolf was not quite mistaken when he replied ingenuously to the charge that his translation of Shakespeare was unreadable and impossible to speak, 'For a youth growing up with this translation, such difficulties of reading or speaking will no longer exist.' Those who grow up with a Bantu language will prefer

---

[1] *Voyage to the Houyhnhnms*, Ch. V.

it to the language of Dante or Goethe. Similarly the use of objects that at first seem repulsive loses its objectionableness when the mind is brought to it again and again. The repulsion wears off. Unconscious compromises are made between earlier ideals and that which is constantly seen or heard. The changeability of human taste in this respect is shown to the point of ridiculousness by the attitude to new and old fashions in clothes. The entirely new often seems tasteless, until it has become the universal fashion. Then it seems natural. Soon after it has gone out of fashion, it is felt once more to be ugly. As time passes, new charms often begin to be seen in it.

As against this it may be an actual danger for a work of art to be too closely attuned to popular taste. This is often the case because critics feel that it is their task to lead popular taste and consequently be always a little ahead of it. They do not like the idea of having judgement similar to their own pronounced by any Tom, Dick, and Harry. They therefore seek new objects for their admiration for which they can act in the capacity of heralds. The number of art lovers is not small that can only be persuaded to espouse a cause so long as they appear to themselves in so doing to be avant-gardists. Of greater importance, because much more widespread, is a certain satiety which opens the door to that urge for change which lies deeply embedded in human nature. This danger that one may outgrow one's taste for certain things is discussed by Goethe in a letter to Carlyle dated 15 June 1828. In it Goethe declares that he had busied himself to such an extent with the coming into being of Schiller's *Wallenstein*, with rehearsals thereof and ultimately with performances of the work, that 'this magnificent play ultimately appears to him as trivial and even positively repulsive'. This was why he has neither seen nor read it for twenty years. It is clear that such satiety amongst people of indifferent judgement will ultimately produce a diminished estimation of any work of art. There is thus a tendency for an ebb to set in in those very areas where general appreciation is at a maximum and is experienced more or less without exception by all educated people. Such an ebb could be discerned in the relations of the German public to Schiller, in that of France to Victor Hugo, in that of England to Dickens, Thackeray, and Tennyson. In many cases, as has already been indicated, this was simply a matter of transitory phase, so that Samuel Butler (1835–1902) hit the nail on the head when he said that the 'history of art is the history of revivals'.[1]

Varied receptivity of sociological groups

These things must be kept in view, even at the risk of setting art on the same level as fashion. As a rule the establishment of a new taste is least dependent of all on the fact of its novelty. For the more cultured an individual taste (the sense of the aesthetic values associated with particular considerations), the less is it capable of modification. This does not mean, of course, that the individual taste has not its own development. It is even obvious that it passes through definite phases with a sort of obedience to law. The child's intelligence as it first begins to develop is most easily attracted by the description of familiar day-to-day incidents, usually regarding its own life; when its imagination awakes, without corresponding development of the critical faculty, it gets a taste for fairy stories; with the awakening of youthful urge to activity it finds fascination in tales of adventure; puberty brings interest in the dreamy and sentimental; maturity brings a more realistic make-up; greater experience of life and the growing sense of reality bring a dislike of highly coloured representation of things and a preference for keen and satirical observation over the merely fanciful. Most adults feel the awakening of interest in biography and a diminution at the same time of the fondness for fiction.

But the more fundamentally this process takes place in the formation of individual taste, that is to say, the more the whole man is taken up with literary interests, the greater is

---

[1] 'Handel and Music: Anachronism', *Note-Books*, edited by H. Festing Jones, London, 1912, p. 130.

the probability that his attitude to the relation between art and reality and to artistic means of expression becomes definitely based on principle, bound to particular directives, and emotionally fixed, the less ready he will be for concessions. In the case of the vast majority of men we can observe a certain process of rationalisation of thought, a process which, beginning in the days of their youth, tends to impair the life of their imagination and which, having a kind of disenchanted effect on their minds, diminishes their capacity for enthusiasm and markedly lowers their receptivity to the artist's perception of the world. Such people are in certain respects incapable of progressing beyond the impressions belonging to a period of their lives when their minds were open and receptive to things of this kind. In later years, however, their enjoyment of art is all too often nothing but their own youth which their memory enables them to enjoy all over again.

The greatest creative artists and the greatest revolutionaries of history form no exception here but remain set in their respect for the achievements which they admired in adolescence and which they had actually been educated to appreciate. Often it takes much time for that respect to disappear; in some cases it never disappears at all. It is indeed astonishing how often it is the great poets themselves who look reverently upward to their predecessors whom posterity not only ranks well below their level but regards as their artistic antipodes. Thus it seemed to Rousseau an act of extraordinary daring when he placed his *Nouvelle Héloïse* next to the *Princesse de Clèves*, the heroically gallant novel of Madame Lafayette; thus throughout his life Byron continued to worship the neo-classicistic work of Pope to which positively divine honours were accorded in the century in which he himself had been born. The strength of this department of impressions gathered during school years upon even the greatest and freest of spirits is nowhere more clearly shown than in the case of Martin Luther, who declared that 'a page of Terence', whom he had had to study at school, was worth more than all the dialogues of Erasmus put together. But let us consider our own case. How difficult we find it to pronounce a critical judgement on poems which we have learnt in childhood. How easy it is for our feelings to overcome any desire that our reason may entertain for a fair and impartial verdict. Consequently every new art would have difficulty in making its way if it were only able to turn to the old public. For in this public, as has just been shown, while there are all sorts of elements that are attracted to the new, those elements are powerful which are dragged only with extraordinary difficulty out of the old rut.

Often this is not realised. A typical example may make clear the differences in view. Wetz, the historian of literature, gives somewhere this picture of the great revulsion in taste of the eighteenth century shown in the turning away from the intellectual culture of classicism to the free play of the emotions:

> The marquis longs to get away from the excessively artificial magnificence of his *salon*; the French reading public, which for so long has languished in the angular regularity and coldness of classicism, is filled with deep longing for a change; the heart that has been frozen and dried up in the refined and powdered world of pastoral romances, with their precious and unreal emotionalism, thaws and expands under the breath of the glowing emotion that trickles towards it from such creative works as the *Nouvelle Héloïse* and *Werther*.

That is very prettily said, but does it correspond to the facts? The literature of classicism is a part of the life of that period. It is dominated by the aristocratic ideals of living, by form, by a highly cultivated enjoyment of life. 'Life is a comedy', says Horace Walpole, 'to the man who thinks, and a tragedy to the man who feels.' The aristocrat prefers the more pleasing conception; his ideal of life is intellectualised. It finds expression inevitably in the art he supports. His life is dominated by tradition, which in his view is bound to be powerful because his whole existence is dependent on inheritance. Property, which is a further condition of his existence, implies a permanent temptation to the enjoyment of life, an enjoyment which is refined by the inherited feeling for form; form acquires further an extraordinary importance from the fact that it is the precise means of social differentiation. This has its influence on art. His characteristic style of living, and the external claims based upon it, further make him anti-individualistic and promote the creation of types. The complete exposure of the life of the emotions, like all that is ruthless in expression, is thus bound to be unattractive to him. It is always revealing things that must at all costs be suppressed.

Thus the aristocrat's only possible attitude to art is that it should serve the decoration and beautifying of life; the exemplary must find expression, and above all heroic achievement, which is the condition of his social eminence. To pass from this creed to an art that, for instance, regards the representation of passions that break down all bounds as one of its important tasks, an art that is in revolt against many things hitherto held sacred, even abandoning the idol of the aristocratic world, social life, to find joy in solitude with nature—all this is not so much passing over to a new taste as betraying the whole existing social ideal and, indirectly, class interests.

In isolated cases this has been done by eminent persons—who will deny it? But they do not establish the rule. Wetz's marquis, who longs to get away from the magnificence of his *salon*, is certainly an uncommonly rare case among his peers. This is impressively shown by historical evidence. How entirely a man like Lord Chesterfield, with his cultured artistic taste, rejected the new trend in art; what disgust Horace Walpole and Lady Montagu showed for Fielding's best work; how the Marquise du Deffand, Walpole's clever friend, railed against the *Nouvelle Héloïse*!

In other times, too, and where the new taste in art does not imply so marked a break with social ideals, we find this resistance to the new and energetic clinging to the old. There are, of course, always striking exceptions. Thus Heinrich von Kleist, for instance, found favour with old Christoph Wieland where he had not found it in Goethe's eyes; thus the Abbé Prévost, author of the immortal *Manon Lescaut*, came from the heroic and gallant type of romance to the homely and sentimental romance of English origin. Both, it is true, were men who had experienced many changes in their lives; Prévost's life, especially, was full of picturesque adventure, and he had often changed his views.

There are others, such as the old Theodor Fontane, and scientists among them—men whose sceptical element is so pronounced that it sees too clearly through the emotional element in their judgement of taste, in all its relativity, for them to remain dependent upon it. But these are essentially exceptions, and must not interfere with our realisation that it is a great mistake to suppose that all that happens is that a taste gives place to a new one. *What happens is not as a rule that a taste is modified, but that other persons become the advocates of a new taste.* Among these others, in great revulsions of taste, another social stratum is directly involved. The history of literature teaches that almost on every page. Only constancy of the social structure guarantees a certain constancy of taste. As mediaeval chivalry went under, it was followed by the poems that incorporated its social ideals; the struggle carried on by the commencing neo-classicism of Shakespeare's day against the people's drama—a struggle through which Shakespeare's reputation certainly suffered severely in the eyes of people of literary culture, if not among the masses— was closely connected, on the other hand, with a growing aristocratisation of society, which found its superficial social ideals better represented in the art of Beaumont and Fletcher. The eighteenth century, again, saw the entry into the literary public in England of the middle class, which until then had been kept away from the fine arts by Puritan prejudice, and this class became the main support of the new art of middle-class romance, which conquered the world from the Thames.

But this traces only a few of the most striking changes. For in reality it is conceivable that endless sociological groups should be segregated. Not always do they show themselves so plainly as in the instances here given. It is possible, for instance, for men, or for women, to become the special representatives of a particular taste. In the Anglo-Saxon countries the novelists frequently complained—more frequently than in Germany—that their public consisted mainly of women, and they attributed to this fact the predominance of love stories and the unrealistic manner, already mentioned, of their narration. This, however, is not a condition of the nineteenth century. Even in the Middle Ages it was often women who made up most of the reading public for romances— simply because as a rule they were tolerably educated and able to read, which was a rarer thing among the men of their class. In the description of a beautiful woman in a Middle English poem mention is made from time to time of the charm of her mouth, with lips so beautifully adapted to 'the reading aloud of romances'. Later, in the baroque period, the romance actually served to kill time for the aristocratic and therefore unoccupied woman. For who but such readers could have the leisure to plough through the dozen or more volumes of the novel of heroic gallantry of the type of Mme Scudéry's *Artamène, ou le grand Cyrus*? But the new sentimental family novel that first followed it also appealed, according to the express statement of its author, Samuel Richardson, primarily to women.

On the other hand, there are periods and categories for which the man's taste is decisive. To these the Elizabethan theatre belongs beyond question; in its public the women had anything but a deciding voice. Wherever, again, satirical features characterise a literary trend, the women's influence is absent. There are also writers whose varied works have found entirely different reading publics for these reasons— which are connected with sex psychology. Thus Byron's romantic and sentimental verse narratives were devoured by a female public, and, indeed, were definitely written for it, whereas his thoroughly cynical *Don Juan,* in which his personality best finds expression, and which is for that reason the most genuine of his works, has always been a men's book. Sterne's *Tristram Shandy* and *Sentimental Journey* show a similar contrast. In Germany, too, certain types of literature have been mainly for women.

It must also be observed that the average age of readers has varied greatly at different periods. This has involved some difference of standpoint. There were periods, moreover, not so long ago, in which the public meant the family circle and attention had to be paid to the growing generation. We must note also the boundaries set up by differences of faith and denominational currents, which sometimes largely cut across the differences of social class. Only when these circumstances have been made plain is it possible to arrive at any understanding of the historical position of particular works. Anyone who does not realise this historical position will be in danger of associating contemporaneous elements that have no real connexion with each other, and thus coming to conclusions that earn the reproach of being unscientific mystifications.

The conception of the taste-propagating type
In many respects the circumstances of the present day differ greatly from those of past centuries; but in the rise of naturalism it has been seen how there, again, the completely new trend in art demanded new men and women, the most confirmed supporters of the new trend being found entirely outside the supporters of the old one. To take a revealing example, in past decades lyric poetry in Germany gradually became the interest mainly of young girls, a thing that could no longer be said of the art of Detlev von Liliencron (1844–1909) or Richard Dehmel (1863–1920). The readers of lyrics grew in number and changed very materially in character. The sociological centre of gravity shifted noticeably. This, however, is the essence of the process that is continually repeated in changing forms. Thus a clear conception of conditions is only obtained through setting out *types of propagators*

of taste. We saw that it is a baseless fiction to talk of a particular period as that of one or another poet, quietly attributing to the general public a taste for him or his school, and thus stamping him as its intellectual representative. In that way violence is done to the facts. Clearly particular groups form as leading factors. Their nucleus is formed by the taste-propagating types. These are the persons who are *bound to be whole-heartedly in favour of the new school because they are in tune with this trend in art.* It completely fulfils their postulates for art. But these postulates are determined by the special character of their whole outlook on life and experience of life. To take the simplest example, the child is in this sense the type that propagates the taste for fairy-tales.

Generally, however, the taste-propagating types incorporate a good part of the environment from which the new trend has proceeded. For sociologically uncomplicated periods, at least, it is manifest that they will mainly belong to the same class, so that we may generalise for past centuries by talking of the taste-propagating type of the courtier or the aristocrat or the priest of a particular kind, and of similar types. But later, too, it will sometimes be possible to identify the type, with due reservations, with a particular professional class, talking, for instance, of the *type of the journalist of the great cities*.

Lichtenberg, with his cool sense of reality, has made certain observations on this subject which we can all study with profit. He once says that since his years at the University he had noticed the difference in the characters of those who admired Haller on the one hand and the devotees of Klopstock on the other. The former were for the most part thoughtful people of high intelligence who 'never neglected the branch of study which provided their daily bread'. Most of the admirers of Klopstock were quite dreadful people (*unausstehliche Pinsel*) 'who loathed the studies they were supposed to pursue. If they were law students, they learned nothing; if theologians they became preachers quite prematurely . . . I never met any medical students who were Klopstock-enthusiasts.' And after observing that 'it is quite well known that Klopstock-admirers are among the Nation's biggest fat-heads' the roguish fellow adds with an air of complete inno-cence 'the facts are as stated, I cannot explain them'.[1] We need not take these observations too seriously, particularly in so far as they are coloured by a certain antipathy, which in the case of Lichtenberg is understandable enough, since he was himself a sort of antitype to Klopstock. Nevertheless this attempt to put a finger on the mentality of particular profes-sions is of some importance. Something of much the same kind happened once before in the literary history of Germany. I refer to the very bold attempt at such an analysis in the defence put out by Karl Gutzkow (1811–1878)—who had received something less than justice from the critics—under the title of *Dionysius Longinus* (1878). This document seeks to unmask those who followed a recent fashion, which had turned its critical utterances against himself, as sometime 'errand boys' (*Handlungsdiener*). Emil Kuh, and Adolf Stern, the Hamburg circle around Hebbel, amongst others even Gervinus, are described in this forgotten dissertation as 'dis-ciples of Mercury' whose service is said to have left its traces in the whole of their thought. One tends to smile at this at-tempt to explain matters away, born as it was of a certain irritation that in all conscience is easy enough to understand. It is certainly not easy to believe that a mercantile mentality can be identified in the Gutzkow fashion as a 'character in-delibilis' nor in the final analysis can we accept the definition of this character as consisting of a lack of humour combined with pedantry and a general dullness of feeling. Nevertheless it remains impossible to deny that Gutzkow has really broken new ground and is proceeding in the right direction. It is impossible wholly to deny that when a new stratum of society begins to play a part in literary life, the balance of prefer-ences in taste undergoes a change, or, to put the matter differently, it is impossible to reject Gutzkow's basic principle that when an entirely new movement is born, this can be traced to the special mentality of those who further it. Our

[1] Lichtenberg, Dieterich collection, Vol. 75, p. 218.

task is now to strengthen our power of discernment for such characteristic instances of mental make-up. We must, for instance, ask ourselves whether the tendency to avoid all ornaments, which is evident in recent architecture, is not to be ascribed to the engineer mentality which is prevalent among so many people today, the kind of mentality, natural enough in a technical age, which sees the highest form of beauty in a strictly functional character and which carries the principles that are self-evidently right in a machine into the exterior and interior of a building. The present age gives ample occasion for posing such questions as these. It is of course rather difficult to get away from rather crude lines of demarcation. The more delicate ones divide men not by professions but according to the differences in their psychological make-up, the relation they maintain between reason and feeling, their receptivity to sensual charm and to the values implicit in a particular temperament—in short, according to all those matters in which in the final analysis one man differs from another.

An example from my own times will serve to make this clearer. One of the last works of Friedrich Gundolf (1880–1931) was concerned with Droste, and how incredible must have seemed to the admirers of Droste's art the judgement of so keen-witted a man when among all the work of this woman of genius he would recognise merit only in the *Judenbuche* and more or less write off as completely worthless the whole of her lyric poetry and her ballads. But what purpose would be served by arguing in detail about such things? This critic, who was so closely connected with the aesthetic movement and the Stefan George circle, was simply one of the propagators of a kind of taste that was different from that of the devotees of Droste. He applied a different standard since he lacked any organ that could have made him sensitive to this Westphalian poet's vision of the Nether German landscape, to the mastery skill displayed in her portrayal of the gruesome, above all to her moving glorification of ordinary human heroism displayed in commonplace conditions and of the most natural relationship between one human heart and another. This does not, however, imply that in a few decades from now the prevalent evaluation of Droste in Germany will be that of Gundolf whereas our own judgement in the matter will be decried as mistaken. This would happen if our confidence in our own judgement were to lessen rather more than it is in any case likely to do and if the general cultural climate were to be such as to cause a receptivity for this particular kind of art to weaken. For all art—in so far as it does not deliberately exclude itself as 'non-representational' from the kind of influence that for thousands of years has been responsible for its greatest triumph—is nourished by its impressions of life itself. It transforms reality. What moves us most deeply in the latter most powerfully arrests our spirit in the former, but where there has been no actual experience there the conditions necessary for the effectiveness of art have disappeared. Thus a person who no longer knows what a heath is and who has had no direct experience of the gruesome, will be unmoved by a poem like the celebrated one of Drostes 'O schaurig ist's übers Moor zu gehn' (Oh it is gruesome to pass over the moor). But we may go further and say that he who turns his back on human history, he who sees the relation between the sexes or between parents and children in a totally different light, will naturally show little interest when these things are mirrored in poetry. How ancient this wisdom is we can see from Ovid's words concerning that great comic dramatist of antiquity, Menander: 'So long as there continues to be a cunning slave, a hard father, a mean procuress or a seductive courtesan, Menander will continue to live.' Thus the effect of poetry is clearly dependent on the continued survival of the reality that serves as its model. Since, however, the real world is continually changing and since our attitude to things undergoes continual modification, a certain ageing process even in the greatest art is inevitable. The undeniable charm, for instance, exercised by such a figure as Goethe's Gretchen had inevitably to grow less when the feminine wish-image took on another colouring and the naïve character of the dutiful and domesticated maiden began to lose its appeal. Although no defect (till then supposedly concealed) has been brought to light in the artistic achievement, the beholder's attitude towards that achievement has undergone a change. For that reason alone the contemporary beholder has a great advantage over his successor in time. A man who was present at the performance of *Hamlet* at the London Globe Theatre in 1601 must have enjoyed a thousand charming features, of which, despite its enthusiasm for the work, posterity is wholly ignorant.

Of course it will be said that it is of the essence of any real artistic achievement to bring the object nearer to us by the very manner in which it is treated. It is also said that the measure of real achievement is the degree of human grandeur and of sincerity that is attained. Yet our ability to feel warmly about anything is limited by the character of the thing itself, and as for human grandeur and truthfulness in the representation thereof, one can only say that all argument about aesthetic matters would come to a standstill if these concepts could be either grasped or defined. Let us remember that even Shakespeare and Rembrandt were regarded as fairly unmodern towards the end of their lives. If we remember that, we shall be ready to believe that almost anything is possible.

The 'inwardly involved'

The thesis which I have attempted to establish is therefore that art is dependent on certain propagators of taste and that the ability of such groups to assert themselves is again dependent on the degree of power they can exercise within the social structure or, to be more exact, on the extent to which they control the mechanism of artistic life, though the concept of power should not be interpreted wholly in a material sense but also not wholly in an immaterial one. Such an analysis will necessarily encounter violent opposition, and this will start as soon as we even begin to reconstruct the type of the propagator of taste as though it were something constant in itself. The propagator of taste, people will say, who is, so to speak, the substratum of any particular movement or fashion, and whose function is over when these come to an end, may be identified so far as the past is concerned, and such identification may to some extent be attested by the frequent connexions traced by scholars between certain forms of style and a particular way of life. A good example of this is to be found in the concept of 'bourgeois art'. But do we not see by looking around us to-day that the same milieu can beget basically different forms of style? Let us suppose that we could indeed identify a certain clearly recognisable type as the propagator of a certain phase of art and were able to trace that phase to the influence of this particular type; should we thus be in a better position to evaluate the phase in question? Is it not of the very essence of art that it is valid for mankind in general? Are there not works of literature which have been produced under conditions greatly differing from our own by people with a psychological make-up very different from ours, but which, despite all this, contrive to delight us? Is not just this the greatest thing about art, that it need not be tailored to the taste of existing groups but rather creates its own community, and that to such a degree that the great artist can say of himself with John Wesley: 'My parish is the world.'

Yet there are a number of answers that can be given to such objections. First of all a particular taste, in the sense that the word is here used, denotes a relationship to art in which a man's whole philosophy of life is mirrored or at any rate one where the inmost being of the man himself is involved. Nor need it surprise us that where this is not the case, where no sort of comprehensive philosophy of life is implied, as is surely the case with the applied arts or where a particular phase of art does not really touch the depths of our nature, a variety of forms may excite pleasure in the same person one after the other. We are dealing here with a phenomenon which is particularly widespread to-day, when there are so many people with an interest in the arts who are nevertheless not spiritually involved but seem to be merely intellectually interested in experiments with new kinds of media and effects. The fact is that when we are dealing with people's relation to art the possibilities are much more numerous than our histories of literature and of art might lead us to suppose. Such a man as Klopstock, for instance, whose works were placed next to their bibles by his enthusiastic followers, belongs, when viewed from the standpoint of his spiritual function in art, to a quite different category from many of the poets who followed him on to the official Parnassus. In other words, the farther away they are removed from the centre of our spiritual life, the more rapidly changes can take place. Our forms of burial tend to be conservatively maintained, while our fashions in hats continue to change. While therefore contrasting and even sharply contradictory fashions in art succeed one another in the preferences of the same individual, this is nothing other than a most regrettable indication of the prevailing poverty of art so far as its ability to touch human feelings is concerned. We might add that it is necessary to regard such things from a certain distance in time. This is particularly true to-day when a work of art is no sooner born than numerous experts hurl themselves upon it in order to engage in its interpretation, to place it within its proper group, and generally to 'schematise it'. Thus if a man bends closely over a tablecloth he sees the individual spots upon it but not its pattern. We are in the same position in regard to many contemporary cultural phenomena. Many things at the moment appear to us as radically different from each other and yet quite probably we shall at a later date regard them as remarkably similar to each other, once we have attained the distance from them that enables us to see them for what they are.

The universal validity of art
The question of the universal validity of great art confronts us with a difficult problem that cannot be solved by any one single formula. That a poet can contrive upon occasions to hold fast certain profound and yet simple human experiences

in forms of peculiar excellence, and is thus able to affect
individuals in sharply differing periods of time, is of course
a fact attested by all human history. Yet we must ask ourselves whether this may legitimately arouse the agreeable
illusion that finds expression in the oft-quoted words of
Keats:

> A thing of beauty is a joy for ever;
> Its loveliness increases; it will never
> Pass into nothingness,

for have not many 'things of beauty' lost their power to affect
us in the course of time? Also much that in traditional art
can be set to the account of our feeling for authority and even
on occasion to that of downright superstition. Further, the
influence of great historical renown is enormous. Such historical importance can endow with the appearance of life and
effectiveness something which actually has long been dead or
which at any rate—if its 'historical value' is disregarded—
would have little or nothing to say whatever sociological
group was governing taste at any particular time. Unfortunately, such a group does not always possess the courage to
express its negative attitude to greatness which it has out-
grown and so fails to imitate the example of Voltaire when
he remarked of Dante: 'How can he help becoming ever
more famous when nobody reads him?' It is more usual for
such courage not to be forthcoming at all, for when art meets
us, enfolded in the royal mantle in which centuries of adora-
tion have clothed it, every knee bends before its presence.

National differences

Doubts concerning the universality of aesthetic values can be
particularly reinforced by the acuteness of the differences
between one nation and another in their respective esti-
mations of artistic achievement. How does it come about that
something, which, perhaps for centuries, has been regarded
by a certain nation as one of its literary treasures, can on
occasion be permanently refused acceptance by its neighbour, even when that neighbour has inherited a closely

related culture. The idea that great art is international is after all only valid within certain very narrow limits. Rather is that which leaps to the eye the exiguous measure of vital values that the greatest celebrity of one country can sometimes represent for another. To quote but a few of the most striking examples out of a multitude of those lying ready to hand, let us consider the case of Virgil, the feeling for whom in Latin countries is certainly very different from that in the Germanic ones, since the latter feel that he does not in any satisfying degree evoke any depth of human experience. Again the art of Shakespeare has in France—in contrast to its reception in Germany—never produced more than a *succés d'estime*. We might also recall the complete lack of comprehension on the part of so distinguished a man as Hippolyte Taine (1828–1893) for the humour of Laurence Sterne or Charles Dickens. As against this a writer is sometimes better understood and appreciated in a country other than his own, as in the case of E. T. A. Hoffmann who achieved greater popularity in France than in Germany. The explanation must necessarily be sought in the phenomenon described by that monumental mediaeval phrase *Omnia recipiuntur secundum modum recipientis*, which means 'all things are received after the manner of the recipient'. The national mentality, or rather the mentality of the group dominating the artistic life of the country at a particular time, is in one case averse to being receptive, in another it is inclined to be so. That, however, brings us back to the character of the propagator of a certain kind of taste. It is precisely that quality which gives a work of art a special value in the eyes of one large sociological group that remains completely ineffective in the case of another. Even so that which is valid for the nation as a whole and which is accepted without question by it cannot be completely disregarded by the taste-propagating groups which that nation contains.

I am not endeavouring to assert that the appreciation of art is confined within national boundaries as many examples could be quoted to disprove such an assertion. Certainly there are forms of art—and music is their prototype—which are capable of exercising an effect far beyond the frontiers of their country or origin. Where this does not result, the reason for failure need by no means necessarily be sought in any lack of quality of the work of art concerned, but rather in the negative attitude of the person before whose mind it is presented, an attitude perhaps determined by the alien character of the national culture which has called that work of art into being. That such men as Mörike, Hermann Hesse, or Ludwig Richter found no public in the Anglo-Saxon countries is far from stamping them as 'provincials'.

Taste-conserving forces: school and university

Of all the elements that determine taste the school probably plays the principal part. Its instruction in literature must culminate in the aim of awakening the pupil's appreciation of artistic values. This is done by means of examples, and it is only natural, and a principle that has been followed from of old, that the school should make use to this end primarily of the so-called classics, that is to say the works that have won a certain measure of universal acceptance. For the school must endeavour to give instruction concerning the common spiritual possessions, must instil recognised valuations, and must hold aloof from the controversies not only of political but of aesthetic parties.

This does not mean that it must pursue an uncritical cult of the inherited past. But it has not seldom pursued that path. By regarding nothing as suitable material that has not the patina of antiquity, and by refusing to have anything to do with more modern material that was regarded as valuable by wide and important sociological groups, the school has often made its true task impossible. The result in Germany has been growing opposition to youth.

Matters were at their worst in this respect, perhaps, at the time of the rise of naturalism towards the end of the last century. Some sides of this movement accordingly have almost the appearance of a sort of youth movement, and it was by one of fate's ironies that at that time no one was so furiously attacked as the poet whose works shone with the most indestructible youthful temperament—Friedrich von Schiller. He was felt to be a phrase-maker, mainly because the uncritical method of treatment of his work at school, as of literature in general, failed to draw attention to the true artistic values in it.

The reason for this lay partly in the unavoidable circumstance that teaching in this field was not always in the hands of teachers with the sort of gift required for their task; but to a much greater extent it was due to insufficient preparation of the teachers. The spirit of exact research that dwells in our universities sought and found its results in other fields. For centuries the university had claimed to be able to teach the theory of the fine arts, but in the nineteenth century it abandoned this claim to such an extent that a systematic teaching of poetry had become almost a rarity. Philosophy, with a few honourable exceptions, failed entirely to give its assistance. The fundamental principles of aesthetics were no longer a subject of examination. Hundreds of teachers who instructed in German subjects came every year from the universities and yet had never had to concern themselves with questions of the tragic or the comic or the like. Their sense of beauty was entirely untrained.

Apart from this, for some time a sort of odium of the unscientific hung over any sort of dealings with modern art, exactly as if not the method but the object determined the scientific character, or as if there were no discoverable methods for treating the art of recent times. The effects of this state of things made themselves felt not only in the robbing of school work of all interest, the entire lack of reasonable methods of treatment frequently resulting in filling the pupil with lifelong hatred of the classics he had to 'get up', but in robbing the colleges of all influence on literary criticism. The time spent at the University and its seminars passed without leaving a trace on the critics. Nobody has seen the past pupils of any University who have become professional critics show any particular backbone in face of the wildest caprices of fashion that have made their appearance; still less has any sign of an 'academic' school of opinion shown itself in connexion with the academic training. It would be nearer the truth to speak of an entire breach between science and art. In the eighteenth century many of the foremost German poets gained impressions and stimulation from the Leipzig of Professors Gottsched and Gellert that affected their whole lives and work. In the century that followed all this was changed. When, about 1900, the group of ballad writers (Börries von Münchhausen and others) formed round the Göttingen 'Musenalmanach', it was no longer connected in any way with the University.

In some of the conditions pictured at the outset there has of late been an unmistakable improvement. The German universities as a whole still maintain strict seclusion; like many foreign universities, they have begun inviting critics of recognised standing or poets representative of modern art (as Frankfurt am Main; Munich), who may be expected to have a useful influence over young students, to give courses of their own as additions to the purely historical work. The spirit of hostility to the things of the day has gone. There are signs of new developments. Progressive types of school attach much more importance than heretofore to the formation of critical judgement in the aesthetic field, and the effort grows to pave the way for an understanding of the art of our own day. There are even cases in which the pendulum has swung right across, in the direction of an almost entire condemnation of occupation with the literary ideals of past generations. Or schoolbooks appear which aim at entirely changing the centre of interest and at acquainting their young readers with the latest 'literary fashion'. It is obvious that this is completely to misread the task of the school as described above.

On the other hand, it is conceivable that the study of literature would be usefully aided by the encouragement and promotion of individual creative work among students. This would be a return to immemorial school traditions, which for some generations have been departed from, but which, regarded from the right angle, may be seen to contain a very fruitful seed. In spite, however, of occasional initiative in this direction, it cannot in general be said that the school exerts any serious influence over the changing development of literary taste. In regard to literature the school is the guardian of tradition.

Organisations exerting influence: literary societies, lending libraries, and the like

More important for the spread of literary taste are certain institutions, among which are the *Literaturvereine* or 'Literary Unions' which for decades possessed a not inconsiderable importance. That importance has considerably diminished— the Munich 'Tukan' is in this respect something of an exception—as a result of that loosening of social ties to which reference has already been made. The institutions in question may in some sense be regarded as the heirs of such German *Sprachgesellschaften* of the seventeenth century as the Palmenorden, the Pegnitzschäfer, and other associations, which gave place in the eighteenth century to such literary societies as those formed by Bodmer and Breitinger in Zürich and by Gottsched (who reorganised an older form) in Leipzig. These literary societies are associations of not very varied character, mostly led by persons of academic training, and are scattered all over the country. For the past generation or so they have regarded it as one of their main tasks to acquaint the public with the poet in person; they have induced him to give, for a definite fee, readings from his works. In the eighteenth century these readings, then more of a rarity, were called 'Reading Concerts'.

In this way a talent may achieve on occasion a stronger and more direct appeal, and there are cases in which the lasting impression thus created by a poet's personality has prevailed over many hostile or lukewarm criticisms. As, however, for most people the criterion in art consists in a measure of success already achieved, and as the principal witness to such success is, after all, the press, on the whole the literary society serves only to add to the popularity of those who have already become known. It carries on propaganda for the taste of others. Occasional encouragement of local elements can do little to alter this impression of it.

Much the same effect as that of poets' readings is produced by professional lecturers, and recently by the authors' even-. ings arranged by booksellers in the great cities. Among these may be counted certain associations in the great cities, mostly of young writers who are out to bring themselves into public notice.

More and more the influence of the family has dwindled in recent times in this field—the influence of the smallest and at the same time the most valuable of the sociological cells of which the whole organism of the people is made up. The family as a cosy intellectual unit depends on suitable relations of the parents to each other, suitable relations between parents and children, and a common pursuit of culture— conditions which before the eighteenth century were attained only in exceptional cases. The intellectual atmosphere which then developed in middle-class homes grew out of the read-ing of good books usually read aloud in the circle of parents and grown children. Since the middle of the eighteenth cen-tury the father or mother reading to the assembled family has been the typical scene for the whole of Europe. Idyllic pic-tures by such painters as Chodowiecki or Ludwig Richter have stereotyped this scene for succeeding generations. Such a scene is a rarity nowadays. The environment that made it possible hardly exists any longer. The typical 'summer house', in which the pencil of the nineteenth-century artist drew a family sitting comfortably together with their books or listening, a symbol of easy circumstances, has become the privilege only of a few families in the small towns or the countryside; the comfortable leisure hour has become almost legendary. And the very interests of the members of the family are now divergent. Thus the family as a medium of literary propaganda in the old sense no longer exists to any serious purpose. Here as in other fields the former function of the family has been taken over by the community.

Films, radio, and television have forced themselves into the foreground. Book reviews on the radio, because they are more lively and more personal, often attract more attention than those that are published in newspapers. The adaptation of well-known works of literature for the screen certainly serves to enhance the interest of the cinema-going public which previously had scarcely had so much as a veneer of literary education. Workers' educational organisations are doing their valuable work in giving that education, such as it was, a greater depth.

Lending libraries are of great importance for literary life. They date back to the eighteenth century and achieved their first flowering in the Biedermeier Period. Wilhelm Hauff once gave us a lively and gently humorous description of the doings of such a library (1826). There were, he says, about five hundred of them in Germany at that time—there were several in every town—and the great stream of novels continued to debouch into them, for the public considered the purchase of such books as money thrown down the drain. In the picture he draws much instruction is to be gained from the social status of the figures that people it. 'Before I open my shop at eight o'clock,' proudly declares the funny little shopkeeper whom he describes, 'there are whole flocks of Johanns, Friedrichs, Katherinas, Babettes in front of my door because they all must read a few interesting chapters before they do whatever it is they have to do—the young lady before she has her English lesson, the gallant Captain before he goes riding with his squadron, the Frau Geheimrätin before she finishes her toilet.' Though he has a thorough knowledge of of the books he possesses and of his so astonishingly distinguished clients, the proprietor of the little shop never attempts anything in the way of guiding literary taste. In this respect the larger undertakings of this kind which exist elsewhere take up rather a different attitude. Mention has already been made of the influence of the great London lending libraries on such things as the actual work of authors itself. Above all

else they sought to prevent the spread of any kind of natura-
listic tendency. In a pamphlet dated 1885, and entitled
Literature at Nurse, or Circulating Morals, George Moore
bitterly complained that Mudie's Library, which for decades
had been stilling the hunger for reading matter that existed
in every British family, exercised a sort of dictatorship over
the reading public by categorically refusing to take over and
put into circulation any books that smacked of naturalism,
that is to say attempted to deal with the serious problems of
the age. By such methods it was contributing in marked
fashion towards maintaining the taste of its compatriots at
the level of that of an eighteen-year-old girl. Another species
of lending library, the German *Volksbibliothek*, has from the
first acted in a much more positive manner. This institution,
though carefully selecting the books it acquires, endeavours
as far as possible to exercise an educational influence on the
taste of its readers. It is true that the critical observer does
not always remain free from all misgivings concerning the
well-intentioned tutelage it thus assumes over its customers.
Is there no room whatever for any doubt as to the soundness
of the standards that guide its advisers? Insofar as it rejects
rubbish and filth it deserves our respect. But does it never
happen that under the influence of the prevailing snobbery
which has done so much harm to the life of art, it is sometimes tempted to draw all too sharply the dividing line—
which seems only to be drawn in this deliberate fashion in
Germany—between so-called 'great' literature and what in
its opinion is 'merely' entertainment literature, and so damns
a great deal that is and could remain a sound popular diet as
'tripe' (*Plusch oder Schnulze*)?

Not everybody is qualified to engage in such not invariably
felicitous educational efforts. In any case there seems to be a
limit to their effectiveness, for next to such an institution as
the *Volksbibliothek* there is usually a lending library working
on purely commercial principles which nullifies the other's
educational activities by providing the public indiscrimin-
ately with pretty well everything it desires.

In Roman Catholic regions both types of library are out-distanced by the Borromaeus Library, which is more recommended in authoritative quarters and is also less expensive. Its friends are often interested in directly and indirectly assisting the public library to become a sort of scientific auxiliary library, less concerned with satisfying literary needs. This still further reduces its importance in every respect.

The bookseller

It would be like playing *Hamlet* without the Prince of Denmark if in a discussion on the formation of taste we were to omit the retailer. His importance compared with other influences has risen quite remarkably in the course of time. This was confirmed by Compton Mackenzie who in the *Spectator* (1953) told in great detail how the influence of criticism as a means of promoting sales had weakened when compared with that of the librarian and the retailer. (One reason for this according to Sir Compton was the habit in the more recent critics of directing readers' attention not so much to the book itself as to the wit of the reviewer, and unfortunately this most improper practice is by no means confined to the British Isles.) The bookseller is concerned with a more noble form of merchandise than any other merchant, namely with books, and he is thus the aristocrat among traders. If he is to fulfil the high tasks of his calling he must at one and the same time be both a scholar and a business man, i.e., he must combine a thorough literary education with the agility and skill of a good merchant. He must, in fact, be an amphibious being, who is as much at home in the realm of the spirit as on the *terra firma* of the market. The means of equipping him for his difficult profession in all its different branches have been created by far-sighted individuals and organisations and have been progressively perfected through the years. The methods of approaching the customer have been carefully studied and the practical inferences drawn from the knowledge so gained. When after the First World War the so-called *Bücherstube* (bookroom) was introduced which dispensed with all the ordinary arrangements of a bookshop and let customers rummage around as they pleased, this was rightly regarded as introducing a new relationship between the reader and the book. The opportunity for publishers and booksellers to meet together which has now for some years been provided by the Frankfurt Fair, where attention can be drawn to important new publications, provides all those who are interested in things of the mind with yet another new means of keeping abreast of the latest developments.

The Book Societies

Yet another development which is not without importance in the process of the shaping of taste can be seen in the 'book societies' which have assumed such enormous proportions since the 1914–18 war. Their members can be counted by the hundred thousand. In the United States the 'book clubs' grew early to mammoth proportions. The 'Book of the Month Club' founded by Harry Scherman numbered 4,750 members in the year it was started (1926). Twenty years later it had 925,000 subscribers, while the Literary Guild had at about the same time a membership of no less than one and a quarter million. At the same time also the 'Doubleday's Dollar Club' had a membership of 700,000. The American example was followed with equal success elsewhere. In Germany, too, the 'book societies' have vast numbers of members whom they supply with reading matter. Among the books supplied are many older works of established reputation which are delivered in a neat and attractive get-up, a feature on which the members appear to lay great weight. Indeed it is this particular category of merchandise that might well play an important part in shaping taste, if the concerns in question were less determined to maximise sales and avoid all risks. Where new writing is concerned the organisations differ sharply from one another in their literary zeal. The Book of the Month Club in America has set up an entire hierarchy of judges. Several panels, one after another, sift the works to be considered, which number on an average three hundred a month. The work that secures the greatest number of votes is declared to be the 'Book of the Month' and is certain of success. Other clubs tend to associate to a greater degree the actual readers in their choice, in so far as they do not confine themselves simply to the reprinting of best-sellers. It has been shown that these book clubs, which initially had to contend with determined opposition from the book trade, have greatly furthered the reading habit, particularly in small towns and in the country. The strength of the influence they exert on the formation of literary taste is too obvious for comment. Naturally, a totalitarian state will not hesitate to play its part in this department too. It is therefore not surprising that one of the first things the Nazis did when assuming power in Germany (1933) was to attempt to assume the guidance of public taste by proclaiming what were in the Nazi view the 'six best books of the month'. A particularly attractive feature of the latter activity was the distribution of prizes for short and pungent criticisms on the part of the readers. It was, however, with a kind of grim pleasure that the opponents of the system—now silenced and disarmed—could note that at least in this department 'the limits of tyranny had been exceeded'. For after a very short time Herr Goebbels's Reich-Schrifttum-Kammer quietly ceased making any announcement of these 'six best books of the month'. It was becoming apparent that such announcements were sufficient completely to kill the sales of the books concerned.

The objection often raised that an association can create a programme but not art will not impress any who have some knowledge of the history of literature. Think of the birth of neo-classicism in Shakespeare's day! It is not by any means unprecedented for a programme to be drawn up and the soil prepared by its demands, and for the seed of a new art then to fall upon it. The essential thing is that the programme shall not be drawn up from a wholly backward-looking point of view—a danger that exists in certain literary reform associations. This objection soon falls away if art remembers once more that without the representation of that which is of human value it is doomed, and that there can be no true artistry without true humanity.

Final considerations

From our consideration of the elements at work in the deter-. mination of taste there now proceeds a certain clarification of conceptions until now confused. Since beauty cannot be achieved by any process of logic, art does not exist in a world of absolutes and its acceptance is dependent on the character of the accepter, and since the establishment of a taste is thus not independent of sociological forces, which are not always of a purely intellectual nature, it is well not to abandon prematurely one's own judgement in favour of what is assumed to be the *communis opinio*, still less to condemn the former as faulty and regard its rejection by posterity as self-evident. It should be borne in mind that so-called 'faulty judgements' have frequently occurred even among the great creators, who should be particularly discerning on such matters as originality and creative power. Samuel Richardson, for instance, as we have already seen, said of his contemporary Sterne's *Tristram Shandy* that this book represented a folly of fashion which would soon disappear, while Goethe felt justified in prophesying of Wieland's *Oberon* that 'so long as poetry is poetry, gold is gold, and crystal is crystal, it will be loved and admired as a masterpiece of the poet's art', whereas, as everybody knows, he had a very poor opinion of the art of Heinrich von Kleist. It is therefore not, as Shelley tries to persuade himself to believe, the judgement of the stupid multitude that time reverses, but that of very well known and respected judges. It hardly needs elaborate proof to show that professional critics make no better showing when we examine what has survived of that which they condemned and what has disappeared of that which they belauded.

We seldom refer to such verdicts as these without a hidden or even an open reproach for the regrettable lack of understanding they disclose, yet if we examine them more closely we may well have certain misgivings; we may well begin to ask ourselves whether the person who assumes the right to speak of faulty judgements wherever posterity has failed to endorse a particular verdict may not frequently be seeing things in a false perspective. Now it is clear that opinions which, like those I have quoted, expressly refer to the future, have been proved wrong by the way things have actually developed, but their erroneous character is almost inherent in the form in which they have been stated. At any rate it is particularly obvious thanks to that form. The fact is that there is a strong element of uncertainty in all such references to the future. Basically, however, aesthetic judgements need no more refer to the future than juridical ones. The essential thing that they must do is to make plain a certain attitude towards certain facts and tell us what the person judging thinks about them. Now such opinions may be expressed under a variety of conditions. There may, for instance, be a deficiency in the critical faculty in regard to artistic quality. This may be due to a lack of inborn endowment or to the fact that the judgement is unschooled and is thus incapable of adequate comparisons. From such people as these, among whom many persons of excellent education are to be found, it is self-evidently hopeless to expect a sound independent judgement in matters of art, but when Richardson turns against Sterne, when Schiller turns against Bürger, Goethe against Kleist, Gutzkow against Mörike, then we are confronted by something entirely different. Here it is utterly impossible to speak of a deficient critical faculty or of any inadequacy of what might be termed the critical organ or of any insufficiency in the feeling for quality. At worst we can say, if we approach the matter from one particular point of view, that there has been a one-sidedness of taste. For in all these cases their own literary achievements have put the people concerned in a position where they cannot possibly be charged with a lack of such a knowledge of their craft as to unfit them for the function of critics.

Seen from the standpoint of posterity it is quite possible that such verdicts may be ascribed to the fact that their utterers were behind the times. Had these observers of art, many will be tempted to say, been born twenty years later, their verdict would probably have been quite different and they would have approved that which they actually rejected. And yet such speculations are idle, for every individual is for the better or worse the product of circumstances obtaining at a particular time, or circumstances whose nature and effect will never be precisely repeated.

It might well be added that there is hardly anything more tragi-comic than the inability displayed by every generation afresh to recognise that their own artistic conceptions are determined by the age in which they live and the tendency—itself resulting from such inability—to regard their views as capable of maintaining themselves in perpetuity, though the people who will ultimately bury them are probably already at the door. (Note that it is always the other fellow who calls one a reactionary.) A particularly telling example of this has been furnished us by Cornelius Gurlitt in his *Deutsche Kunst seit 1800* (German Art since 1800) in the passage (pp. 250 ff.) which describes how every new movement in the second half of the last century regarded itself again and, again in distinction from its immediate predecessor, as the true representative of the truth of Nature.

In practice the resolution of contradictions is achieved by the process that causes the general trend of things to pass over a certain phase of taste—which means that the propagators of the dominant phase have begun to weigh down their rivals in the scales of criticism.

Two important points emerge from this analysis. Firstly we see the decisive factor, not in some objective value, but in a subjective attitude. This must needs infuriate those doggedly opinionated people whose minds are dominated by the conception of absolute values in any kind of artistic achievement. Secondly there is the fact—and this is what I had in mind when speaking of the weighing down of the scales—

that we are concerned with a sociological process which may be likened to a battle, a battle often carried on with distinctly material weapons. Uncritically to accept the result of this battle, as has hitherto been the custom, without ever bothering by whom or for whom that result has been brought about, in a word to make society in general responsible for that result and simply to account one's contemporaries *qua* contemporaries the representatives of the phase of taste that happens to prevail at the moment—this really will not do at all. On the contrary, nothing will do more to further the interest of the arts, nothing can be of greater importance for their health both now and in the future than that we should realise that in the realm of the mind, as in every other, there is no such thing as an iron necessity for affairs to follow a certain course, but that such a course is determined by the actions of men and that those who passively refrain from action make action possible by others. Like politics, the life of art consists of a struggle to enlist followers. In the realm of taste therefore the first task of anyone who wishes really to get down to the truth is the discovery of points of origin. Who is the active agent behind it all? i.e., whence comes a particular taste? Who are the propagators? What was it that enabled it to assert itself? For nothing can be more disastrous in its effects than the claim, so constantly made, for universal validity of artistic values. Though it is very natural that every achievement should be accompanied by the wish that it should address itself to everybody, though it is most necessary that nothing should be rejected without being put to the test and that people should keep themselves receptive for all things, including those that deviate from the existing norm, the individual must be free to turn his back on anything alien to his own nature exposing himself to the reproach of a 'faulty judgement'.

On the other hand, the recognition that all art rests fundamentally on the shoulders of a particular taste-propagating type should strengthen the critical attitude of the individual and his confidence in himself. If, as shown above, a new taste appearing anywhere is the expression not by any means of the 'spirit of the age' but only of the spirit of a particular group, which may fail to represent the spirit of the age, then nothing is more reasonable than to look closely at this group before bowing to its demands.

At no time, perhaps, has this warning been more necessary than to-day, when even the educated public has so largely convinced itself of its immaturity in matters of art and so widely accepted the idea of the freedom of art—that is to say, of its own divinely ordained dependence upon the narrow world of art cliques and art critics. The courage to have a taste of one's own has very largely disappeared. Only the practice of complete honesty with ourselves, and where necessary the deliberate organisation of the lay public, can lead us to our goal.

INDEX

Index

Index

Index